# Promoted Into Incompetence

*Why Good Workers Become Poor Leaders
and How Organizations Can Change That*

David E. Fraser, Ed.D., MPA

Fraser Leadership Group

Copyright 2026

© 2026 David E. Fraser
All rights reserved.

No part of this publication may be reproduced, distributed, or transmitted in any form or by any means, including photocopying, recording, or other electronic or mechanical methods, without the prior written permission of the publisher, except in the case of brief quotations embodied in critical reviews and certain other noncommercial uses permitted by copyright law.

For permission requests, contact:
Fraser Leadership Group
www.fraserleadership.com

ISBN 979-8-9936905-3-7

Published by Fraser Leadership Group
San Francisco, California

Printed in the United States of America

For every capable professional who was promoted with good intentions—

and discovered that leadership requires learning anew.

In memory of my mother, Maureen Fraser,

whose twenty years of service with the U.S. Social Security Administration

exemplified the quiet integrity and human kindness that define true public service.

# Acknowledgements

The ideas in this book have evolved over many years of teaching, public service, and dialogue with practitioners who embody both the promise and the complexity of leadership.

I am deeply grateful to my colleagues in the Department of Public Affairs and Administration at California State University, East Bay, whose dedication to ethical governance and public stewardship continues to inspire my work. Their thoughtful engagement with the realities of public leadership has enriched my understanding of competence, readiness, and responsibility.

Special thanks are due to Dr. Jay Umeh, Professor Emeritus and former Department Chair, for his generous contribution of the Foreword and for his decades of mentorship and collegial support. I also extend appreciation to the many students and professionals—public servants, healthcare administrators, and nonprofit leaders—who participated in my workshops and seminars. Your candid stories of growth, challenge, and reflection gave this book its grounding in lived experience.

I also wish to recognize the members and colleagues of the Conference of Minority Public Administrators (COMPA) and the American Society for Public Administration (ASPA) communities, whose scholarship, dialogue, and advocacy continue to elevate the standards of leadership, ethics, and equity in public service. Their example and engagement have informed much of the perspective reflected in these pages.

I wish to recognize the staff and leadership of Contra Costa County, whose everyday work exemplifies the courage and moral clarity required of public service. I am also indebted to my colleagues and partners through the Fraser Leadership Group, who continue to support this mission of strengthening ethical and competent leadership across sectors.

Finally, I offer heartfelt thanks to my family for their encouragement and patience throughout this long process of writing and revision. Your faith in the work—and in the purpose behind it—sustained me at every stage of this journey.

# Foreword

In every field of professional practice, advancement brings new expectations. In public administration, healthcare, and the nonprofit sector, those expectations often shift from technical proficiency to the far more complex demands of leadership. Yet our systems still tend to equate mastery of a task with readiness to lead others who perform it.

Having served more than three decades in the academy—teaching, advising, and leading one of the largest graduate programs in public administration in the California State University system—I have witnessed this paradox repeatedly. It is the recurring contradiction in professional life: technical excellence so often precedes, yet rarely predicts, leadership competence. Capable professionals ascend through merit, tenure, or circumstance, only to find that leadership requires an entirely different vocabulary—one built on people, policy, ethics, and judgment. Far too often, they must learn it through trial and error.

Dr. David E. Fraser's *Promoted into Incompetence: Why Good Workers Become Poor Leaders—and How Organizations Can Change That* confronts this paradox with uncommon clarity and compassion. It is at once an analysis of how organizations inadvertently manufacture unprepared leaders and a guide for how they can do better. Drawing upon his dual identity as scholar and practitioner, Dr. Fraser demonstrates that leadership failure is rarely a failure of individuals; it is a predictable outcome of structural and developmental neglect.

I have known Dr. Fraser for many years—first as his professor when he was a promising graduate student, later as a respected colleague and faculty member in our department, and ultimately as a leader in his own right. Throughout that journey, I have admired his intellectual rigor, his integrity, and his deep commitment to public service values. His teaching, writing, and administrative leadership have consistently embodied the fusion of theory and practice that we strive to instill in every student.

This book extends that tradition. It integrates research from across the disciplines of public management, organizational behavior, and ethics, translating it into language that speaks to real institutions and real leaders. The chapters on systemic drivers of incompetence are particularly illuminating—showing how merit systems, internal promotion cultures, and inadequate mentoring pipelines interact to produce avoidable leadership crises. The proposed remedies are equally pragmatic: structured development, intentional mentorship, and an ethic of preparation that treats leadership as a craft, not a reward.

In my view, *Promoted into Incompetence* fills a crucial gap in both the scholarship and the pedagogy of public administration. It reminds us that technical excellence is a foundation, not a finish line, and that the cultivation of leadership must be as deliberate as the cultivation of expertise. For emerging leaders, it offers a candid mirror; for institutions, a blueprint for reform; and for educators, a framework to realign curriculum with the realities of governance and management.

Those of us who have spent our careers preparing the next generation of public servants will recognize in these pages both a challenge and an invitation—to move beyond the assumption that promotion alone confers readiness, and to build systems that genuinely equip our leaders to succeed.

It is with great respect for Dr. Fraser's scholarship and enduring contributions to our field that I commend this book to you.

*Jay Umeh, Ph.D.*
Professor Emeritus and Former Chair
Department of Public Affairs & Administration
California State University, East Bay

# Preface

Every profession has its quiet ironies. In public service, one of the most persistent is this: the reward for excellence is often a promotion that requires entirely new skills—skills the individual was never taught, and that the system rarely invests in teaching.

Over more than three decades as a public administrator, executive, and educator, I've watched technically brilliant professionals—analysts, clinicians, engineers, accountants, planners—move into leadership roles with genuine excitement and sincere dedication. Many succeed admirably. But others, often through no fault of their own, find themselves in unfamiliar terrain: managing people, navigating politics, balancing budgets, and motivating teams under pressure. These are not failures of effort or intelligence; they are failures of preparation.

The seed for this book was planted in the same classrooms, meetings, and mentoring sessions where I've spent much of my career. Again and again, I encountered the same pattern: organizations promoting high performers because they "seemed ready," only to watch those individuals struggle—isolated, anxious, or quietly ineffective—because no one had prepared them for the very different demands of leadership. Over time, I realized this wasn't an individual problem. It was systemic. We were, in effect, promoting competence out of itself—converting expertise into uncertainty.

As both a professor and a practitioner, I've had the privilege of seeing this phenomenon from two vantage points. In the public, healthcare, and nonprofit sectors, the developmental infrastructure that should support new leaders—mentorship, training, and continuing education—often lags behind the complexity of the work. In higher education, graduate programs emphasize theory and policy far more than the lived realities of supervision, ethics, and fiscal accountability. Between those two worlds, a gap opens. *This book exists to close that gap.*

## The Cost of Learning by Failure

Every organization pays tuition for leadership development—either up front through intentional preparation, or later through the costly lessons of unprepared management. The latter is what I call *managerial tuition*: the price of learning by failure. It appears as turnover, missed opportunities, low morale, or reputational damage when new leaders are thrust into roles they do not yet understand. I've seen that tuition paid in government agencies that lost promising staff, in nonprofits that burned out their best talent, and in graduate programs that produced technically capable graduates who struggled with human systems. The question is never whether organizations will invest in leadership development; it is *when* and *how wisely* they choose to pay.

## Why I Wrote This Book Now

We are living in a moment when the public workforce faces a generational transition. Retirements have accelerated; institutional memory is thinning; and hybrid work has blurred mentorship and training structures that once happened naturally. Across public, healthcare, and nonprofit sectors, technically gifted employees are being elevated faster than ever before—often into positions with broader budgets, deeper accountability, and thinner support. The conditions are ripe for what I call *manufactured incompetence*: leadership failure created not by lack of ability, but by lack of preparation.

*Promoted into Incompetence: Why Good Workers Become Poor Leaders—and How Organizations Can Change That* is not a critique of promotion—it is a call to prepare differently. It explores how organizations unintentionally manufacture leadership failure and, more importantly, how they can reverse the cycle. The chapters draw from real-world cases, cross-sector research, and my own experience mentoring emerging leaders in government, healthcare, and nonprofit organizations. Each section is built to do two things: (1) reveal a systemic pattern that undermines leadership success, and (2) offer practical tools for preventing it.

This is a book for anyone who has ever been promoted into uncertainty—or watched someone else struggle after being elevated for all the right reasons. It is for supervisors who want to nurture readiness instead of assuming it; for HR professionals redesigning pipelines; for educators seeking to link theory to practice; and for the many dedicated public servants who suspect there's a better way to grow leadership from within.

## How to Use This Book

Throughout the chapters you'll find short, boxed features labeled *Practice Note*, *Quick Check*, or *Leadership Tool*. These are "in-text tools"—compact applications that help you pause, reflect, or take action as you read. They're meant to make each idea immediately useful.

At the end of the book, Appendices A–C provide longer, print-ready resources:

- **Appendix A – Ten Days of Leadership Reflection** – for structured self-reflection and journaling.
- **Appendix B – The Leadership Alignment Project** – an eight-week applied portfolio exercise.
- **Appendix C – Leadership Alignment Templates** – practical forms and checklists for implementation.

Think of the in-text tools as your *practice moments*, and the appendices as your *fieldwork*—together they move you from awareness to application.

My hope is that this book will resonate with both seasoned administrators and emerging leaders alike. It is not a manual of managerial technique, nor is it an abstract treatise on leadership theory. It is a guide to understanding why good people often struggle after success—and how to build systems that make competence sustainable.

# Table of Contents

Acknowledgements .................................................................................... iv

Foreword ..................................................................................................... v

Preface ...................................................................................................... vii

Table of Contents ..................................................................................... xi

Chapter 1 – The Trap We Don't Talk About ......................................... 1

    A Familiar Promotion Gone Wrong ................................................. 1

    The Confidence–Competence Gap .................................................... 2

    Why We Don't Talk About It ............................................................. 5

    The Peter Principle Revisited ............................................................. 6

    Manufactured Incompetence .............................................................. 8

    A Roadmap to What Follows ............................................................. 9

Chapter 2 – The Real Costs of Misaligned Leadership ..................... 11

    What Misaligned Leadership Looks Like ....................................... 11

    Fiscal Costs ......................................................................................... 13

    People Costs and Erosion of the Psychological Contract ............. 16

    Community and Public Trust Costs ................................................ 18

    Risk, Compliance, and Safety Costs ................................................. 19

    Cascading and Second-Order Costs ................................................ 20

    Early Warning Signals and the Leadership Health Dashboard ... 22

Chapter 3 – Systemic Drivers of Incompetence (Part I) ................... 29

    Introduction – How Systems Manufacture Incompetence ........... 29

    Factor 1: Merit System Structures ................................................... 30

    Factor 2: Promotion from Within ................................................... 35

    Factor 3: Favoritism and Personal Preference ............................... 38

    Leadership Tool: Competence vs. Readiness Matrix ........................ 42

    Conclusion – Putting the Drivers Together (and Looking Ahead) ............ 43

Chapter 4 – Systemic Drivers of Incompetence (Part II) ......................... 45

    From Structure to Development ........................................................ 45

    Factor 4 – Lack of Training and Mentorship ...................................... 46

    Case Illustrations: The Cost of Untaught Management ...................... 50

    Factor 5 – De-Emphasis of Public-Management Education ............... 52

    Why This Matters for Readiness and Equity ..................................... 54

    Systemic Drivers → Developmental Failures → Remedies ............... 57

    Conclusion: From Diagnosis to Design .............................................. 58

Chapter 5 – Technical Excellence ≠ Leadership Competence: Bridging the Readiness Gap ........................................................................................ 59

    The Paradox of Promotion ................................................................. 59

    From Expert to Leader: The Identity Shift ........................................ 60

    The Learning Loop of Competence .................................................... 61

    Core Competencies of Leadership Readiness ..................................... 62

    Organizational Implications: The Hidden Costs of Misaligned Competence ................................................................................................... 66

    Building the Bridge: From Awareness to Action ............................... 68

    Leadership Tool – Building Competence Pipelines ........................... 69

    Conclusion: From Diagnosis to Design .............................................. 70

Chapter 6 – Building Leadership Pipelines with Intention ...................... 71

    From Individuals to Infrastructure .................................................... 71

    Anatomy of a Leadership Pipeline ..................................................... 73

    Cultivating the Readiness Culture ..................................................... 78

    Measuring and Sustaining the System ............................................... 79

Chapter 7 – Tools for Emerging Leaders ................................................. 85

Owning the Learning Curve ......................................................... 85
Essential Leadership Practices .................................................... 87
Building Feedback and Support Systems ................................... 88
Ethical and Emotional Competence ............................................ 90
Navigating Organizational Culture ............................................. 92
Sustaining Growth and Resilience ............................................... 94
Conclusion — From Participant to Practitioner ........................ 95

Chapter 8 – From Individual Excellence to Collective Leadership ............. 97
The Shift from Me to We ............................................................. 97
Building Trust and Psychological Safety .................................... 98
Shared Accountability and Decision-Making ........................... 100
Learning Teams and Continuous Improvement ...................... 102
Ethical Culture and Inclusion .................................................... 103
Measuring Collective Readiness ................................................ 106
Conclusion — Leadership as Shared Practice .......................... 108

Chapter 9 – The Ethics of Leadership Misalignment ......................... 111
Why Ethics Belongs in This Discussion ................................... 111
The Three Dimensions of Administrative Responsibility ....... 113
Responsibility as Agency ............................................................ 113
Ethical Frameworks for Administrators ................................... 114
When Promotions Become Ethical Failures ............................ 116
Ethical Conflict and Ethical Congruence ................................. 118
Practical Tests for Ethical Promotions ..................................... 118
Responsibility, Stewardship, and Public Trust ........................ 120
Ethical Imperative Going Forward ........................................... 122
Conclusion ................................................................................... 122

Chapter 10 – Synthesis and Call to Action ........................................................ 125
    Reconnecting the Threads ............................................................................. 125
    The Integrated Leadership Confidence Framework .................................... 126
    Translating the Framework into Action — The Institutional Imperative . 128
    The Individual Imperative — A Practitioner's Checklist ............................ 130
    The Policy and Educational Imperative ....................................................... 131
    The Moral Imperative — Stewardship and Trust ........................................ 133
    Conclusion — Leadership as a Renewable Resource .................................. 134
Glossary ................................................................................................................ 137
    How to Use This Glossary .............................................................................. 150
Appendix A – Ten Days of Leadership Reflection: Applying the Lessons of Promoted into Incompetence .............................................................................. 151
    Day 1 – The Confidence–Competence Gap ................................................. 151
    Day 2 – The Real Costs of Misaligned Leadership ...................................... 152
    Day 3 – Systemic Drivers of Incompetence (Part I) .................................... 152
    Day 4 – Systemic Drivers of Incompetence (Part II) ................................... 153
    Day 5 – Technical Excellence ≠ Leadership Competence ........................... 153
    Day 6 – Building Leadership Pipelines with Intention ............................... 154
    Day 7 – Tools for Emerging Leaders ............................................................. 154
    Day 8 – Changing the Story ........................................................................... 155
    Day 9 – The Ethics of Leadership Misalignment ........................................ 155
    Day 10 – Final Call to Action ........................................................................ 156
Appendix B – The Leadership Alignment Project ............................................. 157
    Overview and Intent ....................................................................................... 157
    What You Will Produce (Portfolio Components) ........................................ 158
    Week-by-Week Guide (8 Weeks) ................................................................... 158
    Templates (Ready to Use) .............................................................................. 159

Appendix C – Leadership Alignment Templates ............................................... 161

    Template 1 – Leadership Observation Log (Week 2) ..................................... 161

    Template 2 – Stakeholder Map Worksheet (Week 2) ..................................... 162

    Template 3 – Driver Diagnostic Tables (Parts I & II, Weeks 3–4) .............. 164

    Template 4 – Competence vs. Readiness Matrix (Week 5) ........................ 165

    Template 5 – Ethics & Equity Checklist (Week 6) .......................................... 167

    Template 6 – Implementation Roadmap (Week 7) ....................................... 167

References ........................................................................................................... 169

About the Author ................................................................................................ 177

# Chapter 1 – The Trap We Don't Talk About

Every promotion begins with the illusion that performance predicts leadership.

The phenomenon of competent employees being promoted into roles where they struggle is not rare; it is the silent loom upon which the culture of many public service organizations is woven. This opening chapter introduces the trap we seldom discuss: how technical excellence, seniority, or raw confidence often substitute for true leadership readiness. Here, we will set the stage for understanding why promotions so often fail, how organizations unintentionally create incompetence, and why this book argues for systemic solutions.

## A Familiar Promotion Gone Wrong

In nearly every public service organization, there's a familiar story. A high-performing employee—the analyst who produces flawless reports, the nurse who can manage a full ward without breaking a sweat, the engineer who solves the problems no one else can—is rewarded for their skill with a promotion into leadership. At first, it seems like the obvious choice. If they were the best at doing the work, surely they can guide others in doing it.

Yet within months, frustration sets in. Projects begin to stall because the new leader is unable to delegate effectively, mistakenly believing they can do the work better or faster themselves. Team morale dips. The once-reliable high performer now spends long nights in the office, struggling to keep up while trying to fix what their staff are doing "wrong". Colleagues whisper about micromanagement. Some staff disengage entirely, while others quietly start looking for transfers.

This is not an isolated event. It is a pattern—one so common that most professionals in public service can recall seeing it in action. The competent employee becomes the struggling leader. In short, they have been promoted into incompetence. This failure is often rooted in the difference between mastery of a task and mastery of people, purpose, and systems—skills the promoted individual was never formally taught.

### Case — Ready on Friday, Responsible on Monday

This scenario, drawn from local-government IT, is hardly unique. The consequences of misalignment become tangible in practice. Consider the county IT specialist who became the go-to person for stabilizing critical systems. After a high-profile outage, she led the technical fix under intense pressure; the department head promoted her to Applications Manager the following week. On paper, the move made sense: exceptional mastery, proven calm, institutional loyalty.

By month two, the trouble was not code but coordination. She now owned vendor negotiations, prioritized cross-department requests, and mediated conflicts between analysts and operations staff. Her instinct—to jump in and personally resolve the technical issue—meant she neglected work-intake triage, stakeholder expectations, and team development. A patchwork of unvetted commitments built up; a budget variance appeared; two senior analysts disengaged. Nothing about her intelligence or dedication had changed. Only the work had changed: from doing to designing, from fixing to framing, from personal heroics to collective capacity. Without mentorship or a structured onboarding, the organization had converted expertise into stress—and began paying managerial tuition in the form of rework, morale dips, and trust erosion.

*Lesson tags:* Mastery of code does not translate to coordination. Failure to shift from solo heroics to enabling the team. Unstructured promotion creates measurable managerial tuition (rework, turnover).

## The Confidence-Competence Gap

Before we can understand the trap in full, we must look at the gap at its core: the difference between confidence and competence. This section explains why confidence is so often mistaken for readiness, and how organizations fall prey to this error.

The challenge of modern talent systems lies in the ability to identify potential over established skill. This is particularly true in public-sector hiring, clinical ladders, and nonprofit advancement, where the most reliable metric of the past often overrides the complex requirements of the future. Hogan and Kaiser (2005) caution against the pervasive performance-potential fallacy, arguing that the behaviors that predict success as an individual contributor—technical skill, adherence to process, and reliability—are often antithetical to those required for managing people and strategic ambiguity.

This organizational failure to look ahead is enabled by a fundamental psychological flaw that is at the heart of this trap. Further, it is a problem we rarely talk about directly: **confidence is not the same as competence**. Psychologists David Dunning and Justin Kruger (1999) famously described how individuals often overestimate their abilities, particularly when they lack the full skill set required to evaluate their own performance. This Dunning-Kruger Effect helps explain why some people eagerly pursue promotions, believing themselves fully ready, while overlooking the new demands leadership will place on them.

## Overconfidence and the Readiness Illusion

Modern behavioral research shows how this trap persists: high performers internalize praise as proof of readiness. When offered promotion, they accept eagerly, assuming that prior achievement guarantees future success. This is the Readiness Illusion. Managers share the same bias. Supervisors, eager to reward reliability, mistake confidence for capability. The result is a cycle of mutual overconfidence: the employee believes they are ready, the manager believes they deserve advancement, and the organization believes it has cultivated talent—until reality intervenes.

This cycle of mutual overconfidence between managers and HR reinforces the assumption that technical mastery translates directly into managerial effectiveness. This is a fundamental failure of screening. Leadership scholar Tomas Chamorro-Premuzic (2019) argues that modern workplaces consistently mistake confidence and charisma for leadership potential: "We often equate confidence with leadership potential, but in reality, it is competence—the ability to deliver results through others—that should matter most" (p. 12).

In public administration and healthcare, this readiness illusion carries particular risk. Technical experts accustomed to clear metrics must now interpret ambiguity, negotiate conflict, and inspire others. This leadership requires adaptive work—mobilizing people to tackle complex problems by changing entrenched beliefs, not just technical solutions. This process inherently generates resistance and conflict. Heifetz and Linsky (2017) define leadership as a dangerous undertaking that requires leaders to be able to withstand pressure, authority challenges, and personal risk in order to advance an organizational or public mission. This dimension of adaptive, high-stakes leadership is utterly missed by promotion processes that reward technical safety and individual task excellence.

> **Quick Check: Spotting the Confidence–Competence Gap**
>
> The failure to look ahead is not just an organizational problem; it requires personal vigilance. Use these questions to pierce the illusion of readiness:
>
> - Does this person's confidence level exceed their actual experience with supervision, budgeting, or conflict resolution?
> - Have they led people before, or only managed tasks?
> - Do colleagues trust their judgment, or mainly admire their technical output?
> - Is their promotion being considered because they are the best *doer* or because they have shown leadership readiness?
>
> - Would you trust this person to navigate crisis or conflict, not just execute routine tasks?
>
> If more than two of these questions give you pause, you may be seeing the confidence–competence gap in action.
>
> Example Scenario: An analyst who excels at data modeling applies for a Chief of Staff role. When asked how they will manage union negotiations (a key conflict resolution task), they confidently state, "I'll just tell them what the data supports." This response, despite the applicant's technical confidence, is a clear sign that their confidence level exceeds their actual experience in a critical leadership competency.

## Why We Don't Talk About It

If the confidence-competence gap is so visible, why do organizations rarely name it out loud? This section explores the cultural and organizational dynamics that keep the trap hidden. Despite the frequency of this problem, the idea of being promoted into incompetence is rarely discussed openly inside organizations. Several dynamics make it a taboo subject.

- **Promotions as Rewards:** In many public agencies, a promotion is seen primarily as a reward for years of loyal service or technical excellence. To question whether a promoted individual is truly prepared for leadership can feel like diminishing their accomplishments.
- **Cultural Taboos:** Few professionals want to be the one who says, "Our new supervisor isn't cutting it". Criticizing a colleague's promotion risks looking disloyal, jealous, or undermining of organizational unity.
- **Organizational Blind Spots:** Leadership and management are often discussed as if they are a natural extension of technical work. Everyone acknowledges, in theory, that the skills are different—but in practice, many organizations behave as though leadership "just happens" when a high performer takes charge.

## The Cost of Silence: Managerial Tuition and Risk

The silence surrounding this issue allows the trap to persist. For the individuals promoted, acknowledging they are struggling feels like confessing weakness. Instead, they double down, working harder, doing more, and often accelerating the downward spiral. This individual struggle is silently permitted by the organization, resulting in wasted time, lost productivity, and the eventual fiscal cost of replacing or reassigning a failed leader (a cost we will examine in detail in Chapter 2).

New leaders *do* learn—but the organization pays managerial tuition in the meantime. This price shows up as turnover, initiative fatigue, compliance gaps, and public trust slowly worn thin. Those are not private growing pains; they are collective liabilities borne by teams and communities.

When this failure occurs, the institution is not merely under-investing in a person; it is structuring future costs into its operations. Two immediate signals predict this risk:

- **Silence around new authority.** The first days pass without explicit coaching on delegation, performance conversations, and fiscal trade-offs. This silence prevents the crucial transfer of tacit management knowledge (Chapter 4), leaving the leader isolated and unprepared for the strategic complexities of the role. The organizational cost of this silence is the delayed identification of operational risks and the perpetuation of the confidence-competence gap.
- **Heroic workload patterns.** The promoted leader spends more time rescuing tasks than designing systems that prevent rescues. This behavior—substituting personal effort for necessary process change—is unsustainable and creates chronic risk. It leads directly to the staff burnout and exhaustion that fuels the high turnover rates quantified in Chapter 2.

## The Peter Principle Revisited

The idea that people rise to their level of incompetence is not new. The concept gained popular, albeit satirical, resonance decades ago when Laurence J. Peter and Raymond Hull (1969) captured it half a century ago in *The Peter Principle*, observing that "In a hierarchy every employee tends to rise to his level of incompetence" (p. 25). Peter's work was satirical, yet it exposed an enduring truth: performance in one job is often a poor predictor of success in the next. Peter's observation has survived because the underlying mechanism never changed—promotions still rely more on retrospective performance than prospective capability.

The Peter Principle was not merely a quip about individuals; it was an early systems critique. The problem today is that this paradox has evolved into something more systemic: organizations unintentionally manufacture incompetence through the very processes designed to reward excellence. This structural misalignment is the flaw that the book's solutions must correct.

## An Old Problem in a New Context

While the core observation—that performance in one job is a poor predictor of success in the next—is old, the modern context in which this failure occurs is new. Today's public service, healthcare, and nonprofit organizations face pressures Peter could not have imagined:

- **Tighter budgets** that magnify the cost of leadership mistakes. A leader's fiscal misstep that once required a minor internal audit now risks high-profile cuts to essential public services.
- **Greater scrutiny** from media and communities that make leadership failures more visible. The news cycle and social media mean a localized failure can instantly become a crisis of public confidence.
- **More complex demands**—from public health emergencies to intergovernmental coordination—that require leaders to balance technical knowledge with political and ethical judgment. The ability to execute a task is meaningless without the wisdom to navigate stakeholder conflicts.

Furthermore, leadership today often requires adaptive work—mobilizing people to tackle complex problems by changing entrenched beliefs, not just technical solutions. This process inherently generates resistance and conflict. Heifetz and Linsky (2017) define leadership as a dangerous undertaking that requires leaders to be able to withstand pressure, authority challenges, and personal risk in order to advance an organizational or public mission. This dimension of adaptive, high-stakes leadership is utterly missed by promotion processes that reward technical safety and individual task excellence.

In this environment, a promotion gone wrong isn't just inconvenient; it can be catastrophic. The Peter Principle offered a satirical but undeniable diagnosis. This book takes that historical insight seriously but refuses to stop at the diagnosis. The problem today is that we have become fatalistic, accepting the rise to incompetence as an inevitability. Instead, the modern context demands a proactive thesis: How do we stop creating incompetence in the first place? And, crucially, when people have already been promoted without preparation, how do we support them to succeed rather than fail?

> **Practice Note — Spotting the Readiness Illusion**
>
> The cost of this illusion is too high to ignore. Use candid, objective questioning to pierce the veil of mutual overconfidence:
>
> - Probe learning, not laurels. Ask: *What leadership skills are you actively building now, and how are you practicing them?*
> - Test help-seeking. Ask: *Whom would you call for candid feedback on a difficult personnel decision?*
> - Look for system thinking. Ask: *If you could redesign one workflow to reduce rework by 20%, what would you change and why?*
>
> If the answers focus on *solo problem-solving* rather than *enabling others*, you may be rewarding yesterday's competence for tomorrow's job.

## Manufactured Incompetence

Leadership struggles can be framed as a matter of individual weakness, but this narrative is incomplete. We must look deeper at the systems that create these struggles. In most cases, incompetence is not natural; it is manufactured.

Organizations create it by structuring promotions in ways that reward the wrong criteria: seniority over suitability, confidence over competence, favoritism over fairness, and technical prowess over leadership readiness. Hogan and Kaiser (2005) remind us that leadership effectiveness is best understood not as a matter of innate traits, but as a function of how organizations select, prepare, and support their leaders. This synthesis confirms that the confidence-competence gap is a two-way trap: individuals enter it, and organizations fail to screen for it.

The process of manufactured incompetence is not accidental; it is predictable. The "organizational machinery" that produces failure involves several components, which are the subject of the next three chapters:

- **Flawed Metrics:** Relying on technical exams and tenure metrics that measure past individual performance rather than future strategic capacity (Chapter 3).

- **Structural Gaps:** Failing to build pipelines or require multimodal training and mentorship, leaving new leaders to improvise critical people skills (Chapter 4).
- **Cultural Blindness:** Allowing the taboos of silence and the myth of instinct to shield flawed promotion processes from ethical and performance-based scrutiny (Chapter 9).

The trap of being promoted into incompetence is therefore not about personal failings. It is a systemic failure that affects individuals, teams, and entire institutions.

## A Roadmap to What Follows

Before we move into the detailed drivers of the problem, it is important to preview the journey ahead. The chapters that follow will build on this foundation.

- **Chapter 2** explores the real costs of leadership misalignment, both human and organizational.
- **Chapters 3 and 4** analyze the five systemic drivers that create incompetence: the merit system, promotion from within, favoritism, lack of training and mentorship, and the de-emphasis of public management education.
- **Chapter 5** highlights the essential difference between technical excellence and leadership competence.
- **Chapters 6 and 7** provide solutions, from building intentional pipelines to equipping individuals with tools to grow into leadership.
- **Chapter 8** closes with the central lesson: awareness plus intention equals stronger leadership.
- **Chapter 9** explores the ethical implications of leadership misalignment—because promoting someone without preparation is not just inefficient, it is ethically negligent.

## Conclusion: Changing the Story

The trap we don't talk about is both real and pervasive. Yet it is not inevitable. By confronting the confidence–competence gap, recognizing the silence that surrounds it, and acknowledging the organizational systems that produce it, we can begin to change the story. This book is not about tearing down leaders who are struggling. It is about helping organizations and individuals recognize the trap, avoid it, and build pathways to competent, ethical, and effective leadership. The next chapters show how competence can be deliberately engineered—one leader, one system, one culture at a time.

# Chapter 2 – The Real Costs of Misaligned Leadership

> The cost of misalignment is measured in trust, morale, and lost potential.

Leadership failures are not abstract; they carry measurable consequences. When the wrong people are promoted—or when competent people are promoted without preparation—the costs ripple outward through organizations and into the communities they serve.

Misalignment begins quietly. It starts when confidence outpaces competence, when promotions reward technical mastery rather than readiness, and when the organization mistakes movement for progress. The impact of these errors is cumulative.

This chapter explores those costs: operational, fiscal, human, reputational, and systemic. By naming them clearly, we begin to see that preventing leadership misalignment is not just a matter of organizational survival, but a core component of effective public stewardship.

Leadership misalignment rarely happens by accident. It is the predictable by-product of systems that reward technical excellence and visibility while under-investing in supervision, fiscal stewardship, and people development. In other words, we elevate for what was measurable yesterday and then expect competence in what becomes consequential tomorrow. This chapter counts the costs of that gap—not to assign blame to individuals, but to surface the organizational choices that create it.

## What Misaligned Leadership Looks Like

Having seen why the trap occurs, we now measure its cost. The symptoms of misaligned leadership are rarely subtle. They quickly manifest in the daily friction of organizational life. Teams experience micromanagement from a supervisor who cannot trust delegation, or they endure long stretches of indecision while a new manager hesitates to act. Budgets are missed because the newly promoted leader does not understand financial oversight. Staff meetings dissolve into confusion because the supervisor cannot set clear priorities.

These are not isolated quirks of personality; they are signs of systemic misalignment—competent individuals elevated into roles for which they were not prepared. The consequence is predictable: frustration for the leader, disengagement among the staff, and declining performance for the organization

A useful way to frame the problem is through symptoms and their upstream causes:

- **Endless rework of reports** often signals unclear role expectations or the new leader's inability to shift focus from technical details to strategic direction.
- **High staff turnover** may stem from unmanaged conflict, lack of effective support, or a breakdown in the psychological contract between the worker and the organization (Rousseau, 1995)
- **Slow decision-making** can point to a leader promoted without exposure to strategic thinking or comfort with ambiguity.

By mapping these common symptoms to their likely causes, organizations can begin to recognize when a struggling leader is not failing personally but has been set up to fail structurally. When symptoms repeat across units—rework, churn, and indecision—it's a signal that the issue isn't personality; it's pipeline. Recognizing patterns early allows organizations to intervene before damage compounds. If you are seeing the same three issues recur across multiple cycles, treat it as a leadership pipeline problem first, not an individual motivation problem.

## Service-Delivery and Operational Costs

One of the most immediate and tangible impacts of misaligned leadership is on service delivery. This is the cost that citizens, patients, and stakeholders feel most acutely. In a county planning department, permits take longer to process, delaying critical construction projects. In a public hospital, clinic wait times grow because scheduling is mismanaged or supply chain processes are poorly overseen. A critical grant-funded initiative might miss its reporting deadline, immediately jeopardizing future renewal and continuity of service.

These failures carry significant operational and reputational costs. When leadership falters, service delays ripple outward: citizens complain, partner agencies grow frustrated, and elected officials apply pressure. The problem shifts from an internal HR issue to an external legitimacy crisis.

Practitioners must use data to diagnose leadership gaps, not just gossip. A dedicated dashboard tracking key service metrics offers the necessary objectivity, focusing on:

- **Average processing time** for permits, cases, or benefits applications.
- **Backlog volume and aging**—a growing volume of old, unresolved cases is a direct indicator of poor workload management and delegation.
- **Right-first-time percentage**—the ratio of work completed successfully without requiring significant rework.
- **Service-level agreement compliance** (internal and external).

*Tip*: A sharp spike in backlog aging—the average time open cases have been awaiting action—is often the first warning sign of leadership misalignment, signaling a failure to shift from doing to managing the flow of work.

## Fiscal Costs

For the practitioner, the lesson is clear: leadership gaps directly impact the budget's bottom line. Leadership gaps also have direct, quantifiable fiscal consequences that extend far beyond the leader's salary. A new supervisor, uncertain about workload management, may authorize excessive overtime rather than delegating, sending payroll costs soaring. A manager inexperienced with procurement and contract management may allow scope creep in a vendor contract, leading to costly change orders and unbudgeted expenses.

Even more costly are the hidden drains:

- **Staff Turnover:** This is arguably the largest single fiscal cost. Research shows that replacing an employee can cost between 50% and 150% of that person's annual salary, depending on their role complexity (Cascio, 2006). These costs include recruitment fees, time spent interviewing, loss of productivity during the vacancy, and onboarding/training the replacement.
- **Rework and Errors:** The time spent by competent staff correcting the mistakes or unclear directions of an unprepared leader is a direct, unbudgeted expenditure.

When overtime premiums, onboarding costs, and missed deadlines are added, the financial burden compounds quickly. This is an essential lesson: the principle of accountability extends to the financial impact of the hiring process itself.

## The True Cost of Fiscal Incompetence

The failure of fiscal oversight is a core competency failure detailed in Chapter 5. It costs organizations in two major ways:

1. **Direct Budget Overruns and Mismanagement:** A new supervisor, uncertain about workload management, may authorize excessive overtime rather than delegating. A manager inexperienced with procurement and contract management may allow scope creep in a vendor contract.
2. **Strategic Opportunity Costs and Lost Innovation:** This strategic cost—the price of lost innovation or a deferred grant application—is rarely captured on a budget sheet but often dwarfs visible overruns. A leader competent in technical execution but fearful of strategic financial planning will consistently sacrifice future opportunity for present-day certainty.

## Numerical Illustration: The Turnover Multiplier

Consider a regional agency with 120 employees and an average salary of $70,000. Drawing on Work Institute (2023) data, if a single unprepared manager drives just five unnecessary departures per year, the organization incurs roughly **$115,000 in avoidable cost** in replacement cost alone. A more detailed spiral reveals the escalating cost:

- Replacement cost (5 staff X 33% of salary): $115,500.
- Overtime to cover vacancies (1,000 hours at $55/hr): $55,000.
- Rework to fix avoidable errors (300 hours at $45/hr): $13,500.
- One unit, one year: $184,000 in avoidable costs.

Even conservative assumptions reveal how small performance gaps become budget events.

## Leadership Tool: Back-of-the-Envelope Cost Calculator

Public managers can quickly justify investment in leadership training by calculating the costs they are currently incurring:

*Table 2.1 – Cost Calculator*

| Cost Element | Calculation Formula |
|---|---|
| Turnover Cost | 0.5–1.5 X Annual Salary |
| Overtime Premium | Total OT Hours X (Hourly Rate X 1.5) |
| Rework Cost | Rework Hours X Average Hourly Rate |
| External Fees | Invoiced Costs tied to Leadership Gap |

Warning: Multiply the turnover cost by 2–3 if multiple staff leave due to morale decline, as the cost quickly escalates into hundreds of thousands of dollars

# People Costs and Erosion of the Psychological Contract

Beyond dollars and process, misaligned leadership exacts a heavy toll on people. Employees working under unprepared leaders report lower morale. Some feel micromanaged (because the leader is still focused on *doing*), others feel unsupported (because the leader doesn't know how to advocate), and many are left adrift without clear direction.

Over time, this fosters burnout and disengagement. Disengaged employees are less productive and more likely to leave. The departure of high performers weakens the organization further, as institutional memory is lost and the remaining staff absorb heavier workloads.

## The Broken Psychological Contract, Moral Injury, and Inequity

The core human cost is the rupture of the psychological contract—the unwritten expectations between employer and employee (Rousseau, 1995). When a leader is promoted based on favoritism or seniority (Chapter 3) and then proves incapable (Chapter 5), the implicit promise of merit is broken. This failure can lead to moral injury—the distress that arises when one's work violates personal or professional values due to systemic failure—and learned helplessness, which is fostered when employees stop offering ideas because they know initiative won't survive managerial churn or paralysis. Engagement doesn't merely fall; it calcifies, and so does performance. This corrosive combination is a hallmark of misaligned leadership. This failure creates an organizational dependency, where managers who struggle with delegation unintentionally train their teams to wait for specific, micro-level instruction.

A simple, high-trust repair is to require every first-line leader to hold one documented "remove a barrier" 1:1 per week for eight weeks. Track the barriers removed. The signal to staff: leadership exists to enable work, not merely audit it. This intentional intervention counters the cynicism embedded by learned helplessness.

## Equity Implications

Crucially, the impacts are not evenly distributed. Employees from underrepresented groups often feel the effects more acutely, especially when mentorship is lacking or pre-existing organizational bias goes unchecked. Poor leadership can therefore deepen systemic inequities. They receive fewer high-quality assignments, shoulder more cleanup work, and are more likely to transfer out or exit. Over time, this creates a selective attrition pattern: the organization loses precisely the people it aims to retain, weakening diversity and institutional competence. Correcting misalignment is therefore not just a performance agenda; it is an equity agenda. When promotion systems are clarified, and mentoring is formalized (Chapter 6), organizations consciously dismantle the mechanisms that perpetuate structural disadvantage.

Monitoring internal workforce metrics provides objective insight into the human cost:

- **Engagement scores** (often the first measure to drop).
- **Sick leave utilization** (a proxy for stress and burnout).
- **Grievance rates** (filed via collective bargaining units or directly).
- **Internal transfer requests** (staff attempting to escape the misaligned unit).
- **Vacancy fill time** (high turnover units become increasingly difficult to staff).

**Insight**: An uptick in sick leave coupled with a rise in transfer requests is a common early indicator of burnout under misaligned leadership.

## The Hidden Emotional Ledger

Beyond stress and disengagement lies burnout—what Maslach and Leiter (2022) describe as the chronic erosion of the relationship between people and their work. This condition is amplified by moral injury, which is the harm employees feel when they must uphold professional standards within systems that make doing the right thing unusually difficult. This corrosive combination is a hallmark of misaligned leadership. Staff are often fully competent but are continually undermined by managerial paralysis or micromanagement.

Over time, staff who repeatedly watch preventable problems go unaddressed develop learned helplessness: they stop proposing improvements because experience has taught them that initiative won't survive managerial churn. Engagement doesn't merely fall; it calcifies, and so does performance. This failure creates an organizational dependency, where managers who struggle with delegation unintentionally train their teams to wait for specific, micro-level instruction

## Community and Public Trust Costs

The human costs felt internally inevitably spill outward, impacting public perception. When leadership fails inside an organization, the public eventually notices. A faltering agency generates complaints at public meetings. Local media highlight failures, amplifying reputational damage. Elected officials call for accountability, often adding new reporting requirements or oversight that increases workload without addressing the underlying leadership gap.

Citizens do not experience these failures as managerial problems; they experience them as broken promises. They see delayed benefits, stalled community projects, and unmet expectations. Trust in government and nonprofit institutions—already fragile in many contexts—erodes further, creating a significant crisis of public legitimacy. This cost is arguably the hardest to recover from, as public trust is the essential currency of public service.

To track this, leaders should monitor:

- **Volume of complaints** to elected officials or agency heads.
- **Media mentions** (tracking both the tone and frequency).
- **Public meeting escalations** (the frequency of items being pulled from consent agendas for debate).
- **Survey results** on trust and confidence in government services.

Citizens don't see misalignment as a staffing story; they experience missed inspections, delayed approvals, and inconsistent service. Once trust erodes, elected officials add oversight, which adds reporting burden, which reduces time to manage, which further erodes results. The cycle is self-reinforcing until leadership capacity is rebuilt.

## Risk, Compliance, and Safety Costs

Misaligned leadership translates directly into increased risk, compliance breakdowns, and safety failures. When leaders are unprepared to oversee complex systems, the organization becomes more vulnerable on multiple fronts.

**Compliance.** Audit findings multiply when inexperienced managers fail to implement and maintain internal controls. Corrective actions often sit unresolved for months, exponentially increasing liability. Beyond the immediate cost of fines or penalties, repeat findings can place an organization on a "watch list," triggering heightened oversight and stricter reporting requirements. In turn, this can slow program approvals, reduce grant competitiveness, and even jeopardize eligibility for federal or state funding streams. Repeat audit findings are rarely technical mysteries; they are leadership behaviors in disguise—missed follow-through, unclear ownership, and absent coaching on process reliability. Treat corrective actions like project deliverables with a single accountable owner, a standing review cadence, and a published burn-down of open items.

**Safety.** In healthcare settings, leadership gaps can contribute directly to preventable incidents: medication errors, incomplete documentation, staff working without proper licensure checks, or lapses in infection control. Each near-miss represents not only potential patient harm but also exposure to malpractice claims and accreditation risk. In public works departments, safety compliance may lapse, resulting in avoidable workplace injuries, workers' compensation claims, or violations of Occupational Safety and Health Administration (OSHA) standards. Even in administrative settings, insufficient oversight of cybersecurity protocols or records retention policies can create legal and reputational exposure.

Every audit exception, citation, or safety incident carries operational and reputational damage. Regulators and funders quickly label an organization with recurring problems as unreliable, jeopardizing future grant funding or accreditation. To monitor this, leaders must treat corrective actions like project deliverables with a single accountable owner, a standing review cadence, and a published burn-down of open items.

## Cascading and Second-Order Costs

The costs of misaligned leadership rarely stop at the first level. The lack of follow-through and organizational fatigue create deeper, systemic problems that unfold over months and years.

**Initiative fatigue.** Staff grow weary of new projects that stall or collapse because the unprepared leader cannot sustain momentum. Promising initiatives lose credibility quickly, and employees learn to protect themselves by withholding effort on "the next big thing."

**Change cynicism.** Failed projects create skepticism that future reforms will succeed. Staff may quietly resist new directions, defaulting to a "this too shall pass" mindset. Once embedded, cynicism becomes a cultural trait that is difficult to reverse.

**Cross-agency breakdowns.** Public service depends heavily on collaboration. When one partner agency consistently fails to deliver—missing deadlines, failing to share data, or underperforming on joint grants—relationships suffer. Other agencies reallocate resources, partners avoid collaboration, and intergovernmental trust erodes. A reputation for unreliability can effectively sideline an agency from future regional or cross-sector efforts.

**Lost opportunities.** Beyond visible failures, the deeper loss lies in what never happens. Valuable grant funding is left on the table because proposals lack credible leadership. Strategic partnerships dissolve when confidence fades. Innovations are deferred or abandoned because momentum collapses. These opportunity costs are rarely captured on a balance sheet, yet they can dwarf visible budget overruns.

The cascading impact illustrates the profound opportunity cost of leadership misalignment: not just what is lost today, but the potential value that never comes to fruition. Once credibility is compromised—whether with staff, partners, or funders—it can take years of consistent performance to rebuild.

These patterns are not abstract. The long-term costs of misaligned leadership often reveal themselves most clearly when organizations lose opportunities that once seemed secure. The following example illustrates how unresolved compliance gaps cascaded into lost funding and lasting reputational damage.

**Case: The Health Department That Lost Its Grant**

A mid-sized county health department was awarded a multi-year federal grant to expand maternal health services. Within the first two years, auditors noted repeat findings: missing documentation for subcontractors, inconsistent timekeeping on grant-funded staff, and corrective actions left unresolved for more than a year. Leadership turnover compounded the problem. The new program manager—promoted for technical expertise but with no prior supervisory experience—struggled to implement controls and underestimated the importance of timely responses.

By year three, the federal agency placed the grant on "high-risk status," requiring additional monthly reporting and imposing restrictions on drawdowns. Staff morale suffered as administrative burdens mounted. When the next funding cycle came around, the county's application was denied—not for program quality, but because of its risk designation.

The opportunity loss was staggering. A $2.5 million program collapsed, community partners withdrew services, and the county lost credibility with both funders and residents.

*Lesson tags:* Compliance and stewardship are not just operational tasks; they are leadership responsibilities. When leaders are unprepared for oversight, the price is borne by communities that lose access to essential services.

When one agency falters, regional partnerships stall. Joint grants underperform, data-sharing slows, and multi-jurisdiction initiatives quietly unwind. The opportunity cost—the value of what never gets built—rarely shows on a ledger, but it shapes public outcomes for years.

# Early Warning Signals and the Leadership Health Dashboard

Organizations don't have to wait until costs have fully accumulated—until a project is irrevocably stalled or three high performers have walked out the door—to recognize trouble. The failure of leadership, while systemic in its root cause, is rarely a sudden event; it's a gradual erosion preceded by clear, observable indicators. Early warning signals appear quickly when a leader is struggling: cancelled one-on-one meetings, performance check-ins skipped, persistent project churn, and conflicts festering without resolution.

These early signs provide a critical window for intervention. An effective public manager uses data not just to measure past outcomes, but to predict future crises. By recognizing and acting on these warning lights, an organization can shift from a reactive mode of damage control to a proactive strategy of coaching and support.

## Leadership Tool: Leadership Health Dashboard

To move beyond anecdotal evidence and office gossip, organizations need a clear, objective diagnostic tool. This dashboard distinguishes between the Leading Indicators (the early behavioral and operational warnings of a problem) and Lagging Indicators (the visible, accumulated damage that has already occurred). Tracking the leading indicators allows management to address the leadership gap with coaching or training before the high costs explored earlier—turnover, budget variances, and reputational damage—become inevitable.

*Table 2.2 – Leading & Lagging Indicators*

| Leading Indicators (Early Warnings) | Lagging Indicators (Visible Damage) |
|---|---|
| 1:1 meetings skipped or cancelled two months in a row | Turnover above 12% annually |
| Staff complaints rising >15% in a quarter | Budget variance >5% (over or under-spending) |
| Three or more initiatives launched, none completed in six months (project churn) | Audit findings increasing year-over-year |
| Conflict unresolved for 30+ days | Service backlog aging days |

**Action:** Leaders with multiple leading warnings should receive immediate coaching, mentoring, or training before problems escalate to lagging indicators. Ignoring leading indicators is a deliberate choice to absorb future, larger costs.

## Three Illustrative Cases

The quantitative and systemic costs we've explored—from budget variances to staff turnover—lay bare the theoretical failures of leadership misalignment. However, the true gravity of these costs is best understood not in percentages or formulas, but through real-world examples. These cases breathe life into the data, showing how the failure of an organization's selection and support processes translates into daily struggle for the struggling leader, their teams, and the communities they serve.

In the following illustrations, notice how the Leading Indicators from the dashboard became visible problems, and how targeted intervention—focused on the right leadership skill, not just the technical work—ultimately turned the situation around.

### Case: Public Service (The Analyst)

A county promoted its most senior analyst to a supervisory role, assuming her deep technical knowledge would translate into leadership success. The analyst, struggling to shift from individual contributor to manager, viewed delegation as a loss of control and spent time re-doing staff work rather than training them. Within six months, project backlogs grew by 30%, and three of her five direct reports—all high performers—transferred out. The team essentially ceased to function. The county later invested in mentorship and cross-training specifically focused on delegation and conflict resolution. Within a year, backlog metrics improved, and turnover stabilized.

*Lesson tags:* Technical ≠ leadership; unsupported transition; mentorship as corrective.

### Case: Nonprofit (The Executive Director)

A nonprofit program lead was promoted to executive director after a decade of success running a nationally recognized, evidence-based initiative. Once in the top role, she adhered rigidly to the program model that had earned her acclaim. Staff and community partners—many representing culturally diverse neighborhoods—began reporting that the organization had grown less responsive to local needs. Participation dropped, volunteer engagement declined, and donor confidence wavered. A board review revealed that the promotion had centered almost entirely on programmatic accomplishment and grant-writing skill, with little consideration of cultural humility, participatory leadership, or adaptive governance. The board implemented a 360-degree feedback process and launched a peer-learning circle of executive directors to strengthen community accountability. Within a year, participation rebounded, and the nonprofit regained several lapsed donors.

*Lesson tags:* Mission drift through rigidity; cultural humility as leadership competence; participatory governance restores trust.

**Case: Healthcare (The Nurse Manager)**

A clinical nurse manager, promoted for exceptional clinical excellence, inherited responsibility for budgeting and purchasing without any training in fiscal management. Viewing the budget as a secondary nuisance, she failed to monitor expenditures on agency staff and equipment. Within the first fiscal year, the unit overspent by 15%, leading to emergency cuts in preventative programs and deep staff resentment. The hospital had to divert funds from other priorities to cover the loss. Only after mandatory financial training and peer coaching, which helped her understand the link between budget and patient care, did the budget variance drop below 2% the following year.

*Lesson tags:* Budget gap; training intervention; long-term benefit.

## The Ethical Ledger – A Duty of Care

Public organizations steward delegated trust. When they promote without preparation, they breach a duty of care—both to the employees they elevate and to the citizens who rely on their competence. Leadership failure is never value-neutral; it redistributes harm. The costs fall hardest on those least able to absorb them—front-line staff, clients, and communities whose well-being depends on public effectiveness.

This duty of care operates on three levels:

1. **To the Individual Leader.** Organizations owe every newly promoted manager the training, mentorship, and feedback mechanisms necessary to succeed. Throwing someone into leadership "to see if they can swim" is not opportunity; it is institutional negligence.
2. **To the Workforce.** Employees have a right to competent supervision—the same way patients have a right to competent care. Poorly prepared managers create preventable stress injuries: burnout, cynicism, and disengagement.
3. **To the Public.** Citizens fund and depend on these systems. When avoidable leadership errors degrade service, waste money, or erode equity, the breach becomes ethical as well as operational.

Ethical governance therefore demands preventive investment—leadership development as an act of justice. Paying leadership tuition up-front through structured readiness programs, coaching, and mentoring costs less than paying later through turnover, waste, and reputational damage. Preparation is stewardship; neglect is malpractice.

> **Quick Check — Are We Paying Before or After?**
>
> Use this short diagnostic to surface the ethical dimension of resource choices:
>
> - Is your leadership-development budget larger than last year's overtime bill?
> - Do managers receive mentoring before assuming supervisory duties, or only after problems arise?
> - When you discuss turnover or burnout, does the conversation include leadership readiness as a root cause?
> - Are ethical and equity considerations part of promotion deliberations?
>
> If "no" appears more than once, the organization is paying for leadership failure after the fact—and likely at a premium.

## Bridge to the Rest of the Book

The monetary losses, human fatigue, and ethical lapses described here are not isolated incidents; they are the predictable by-products of design choices. They arise from systems that equate technical mastery with leadership potential, that reward confidence over competence, and that treat readiness as optional.

The next chapters move upstream—from these outcomes to their origins. Chapter 3 dissects the first set of systemic drivers: the merit system structures, promotion-from-within norms, and favoritism patterns that manufacture failure before it begins. Chapter 4 continues this diagnosis by examining the developmental vacuum created by a lack of training and mentorship and the de-emphasis of public management education. By exposing those mechanisms, we can begin designing the leadership pipelines in Chapter 6 that honor both performance *and* preparedness

# Chapter 3 - Systemic Drivers of Incompetence (Part I)

*Systems reward technical mastery long before they teach leadership.*

## Introduction - How Systems Manufacture Incompetence

Leadership failure seldom originates with individuals; it begins in the machinery that selects and rewards them. When organizations unintentionally elevate the technically proficient without preparing them for the demands of management, they effectively manufacture incompetence. These failures are not random events; they are the predictable by-product of internal systems that, though designed for fairness, are fundamentally misaligned with the job of leadership.

Technical systems—civil-service exams, credential screens, tenure rules—filter for skill but rarely for readiness. When the selection algorithm prizes specialized knowledge over strategic judgment, a structural flaw emerges. These systemic drivers are living features of how public, healthcare, and nonprofit institutions still identify talent.

This chapter examines three drivers that create what might be called a leadership supply-chain problem: abundant technical expertise but chronic supervisory scarcity. We will explore **merit system structures, promotion-from-within practices**, and **favoritism or personal preference**. Each factor arises from a rational, positive intent but ultimately yields irrational, counterproductive outcomes. The goal is to surface where and how these systems misfire before exploring the critical training, mentorship, and education gaps in Chapter 4.

# Factor 1: Merit System Structures

The public merit system was born in the late 19th century to fight patronage and instill integrity by replacing the spoils system with objective, open competition. Early reforms, notably the 1883 *Pendleton Act,* insisted on objectivity through competitive testing, prohibiting firing without cause, and structuring federal work hierarchically. However, over time, those tools calcified into reliable proxies for technical proficiency—the ability to *do* the work—rather than the capacity to *lead* others in doing it. The "best" candidates in these systems are often those who test well on specific subject matter, not those who can guide others through ambiguity and conflict.

## Merit as Value vs. Civil Service as Structure

For the modern public manager, it is essential to understand the core conceptual distinction that became blurred over decades: the difference between **Merit as an ideal** (a value) and **Civil Service as the administrative apparatus** (the structure). Early reformers defined merit not merely as neutral testing and fairness, but as a passionate moral dimension: a public service character—a desire to act for the broader good, encompassing values, ideals, and ethics.

The Civil Service system is the administrative structure of rules, procedures, and standardized classification designed to govern daily activities. The ideal, or Merit, consists of competence, qualifications, and the absence of political favoritism. Unfortunately, the two became intricately commingled, leading to widespread confusion and dissatisfaction. As the system grew, characteristics designed to foster merit—such as standardization and neutrality—became intertwined with rigid bureaucratic features, which are often the true targets of reform. Even by 1978, President Jimmy Carter lamented, "there was no merit in the merit system!".

The result is that the system now emphasizes protection from specific, negative actions (such as political coercion) rather than proactively supporting actions that advance the high ideal of merit. This historical shift has profound modern consequences: the administrative structure that exists today often prioritizes technical and legalistic compliance over the strategic and adaptive leadership required in contemporary public, healthcare, and nonprofit environments.

## Where the Design Misfires

The fundamental design flaw is the mismatch between the skills measured and the skills required for leadership. The workforce itself has profoundly changed; by the year 2000, specialized technical and scientific positions had dramatically increased, while lower-level clerical jobs declined to about 15 percent of the total classified service.

- **Technical work** is typically linear, individual, and focused on solving concrete problems using established protocols (e.g., following a regulation, designing a structure).
- **Leadership work**, by contrast, is non-linear, collective, and centered on human capital, ambiguity, and risk alignment (e.g., motivating a conflicted team, negotiating a trade-off, communicating vision).

When merit systems only filter for technical prowess, the result is predictable: technical excellence is over-weighted, and leadership capacity is under-measured. A recent OECD (2021) review of public-service leadership frameworks confirmed the persistence of this bias, noting that nearly 70 percent of jurisdictions still rely primarily on technical exams and tenure to certify readiness. The reliance on objective scoring feels safer than subjective evaluation, even when it reliably produces leaders unprepared for the ambiguity inherent in strategic management. Peter and Hull (1969) captured this enduring truth half a century ago, warning that promotion by prior success propels people to their "level of incompetence".

## The Executive Core Qualifications (ECQs)

The federal government's own guidance, provided by the U.S. Office of Personnel Management (OPM, 2023), notes that most qualifying exams "measure what employees know, not what they can lead". To counter this, the OPM developed the **Executive Core Qualifications (ECQs)** to define the leadership competencies required for successful performance in the Senior Executive Service (SES). This framework provides a robust, scalable example of how civil service systems should supplement technical exams with assessments that gauge the ability to manage change, lead people, and build inter-agency trust. This approach positions so-called "soft skills" as hard metrics essential for public leadership.

The five ECQs are:

- **Leading Change** – This requires strategic vision, flexibility, creativity, and resilience to move the organization forward and navigate uncertainty.
- **Leading People** – This involves building inclusive teams, resolving conflict, developing others, and leveraging the diversity of the workforce.
- **Results Driven** – This centers on accountability, decisiveness, problem-solving, and maintaining technical credibility in delivery.
- **Business Acumen** – This requires managing human, financial, and information resources strategically and understanding the organizational budget.
- **Building Coalitions** – This demands partnering, influencing, political savvy, and collaboration across boundaries, both internal and external.

The ECQs attempt to correct technical bias, yet many agencies treat them merely as paperwork rather than a mandate for practice. Until leadership competencies carry equal weight with technical exams, merit systems will continue to certify experts who must **learn leadership on the job**—often at high organizational cost.

**Practice Note: Why Exams Don't Measure Leadership**

Exams are useful for assessing technical knowledge, but leadership performance is far better predicted by multi-method assessment. This approach is not simply subjective but utilizes structured, evidence-based tools. Schmidt and Hunter (1998) demonstrated that multi-method assessment—combining cognitive ability, structured interviews, and behavioral simulations—predicts leadership success far better than any single measure, such as a written test.

For any promotion to a supervisory or managerial level, organizations should require:

- **A structured behavioral interview scored to validated leadership competencies, moving beyond conversational familiarity.** This technique requires candidates to provide specific examples of past behavior, based on the principle that the best predictor of future performance is past behavior. A highly structured interview uses standardized, pre-set questions—often based on the Situation, Task, Action, Result (STAR) format—to probe competencies like delegation, conflict resolution, team motivation, and ethical decision-making. For instance, instead of asking, "How would you handle conflict?", a structured question asks, "Tell me about a time you managed a disagreement between two high-performing subordinates. What did you do, and what was the outcome?" This approach disciplines the interviewer's judgment and ensures that all candidates are measured against the same objective, leadership-specific criteria.

- **A simulated leadership task (e.g., a budget trade-off memo, coaching conversation, or stakeholder briefing) scored with a formal rubric.** This allows the organization to observe candidates *performing* a critical leadership function under realistic pressure, providing a direct work sample that avoids the gap between what a candidate *says* they would do and what they *actually* do. For a public works promotion, this might involve presenting a trade-off memo that balances political demands, budget cuts, and core service goals; for a healthcare manager, it could be a role-play of a difficult coaching session with an employee. The use of a formal, pre-determined rubric ensures that the assessment focuses strictly on the required leadership behaviors (like strategic thinking, communication clarity, and ethical reasoning), making the selection process defensible, transparent, and aligned with true readiness.

The failure to shift from measuring technical knowledge to assessing leadership potential has visible, measurable consequences beyond flawed hiring. When organizations rely on inadequate screening methods, they accept the downstream costs that appear in real-world scenarios. The following three cases illustrate how the blind spots of merit system structures—favoring technical exam performance over demonstrated leadership readiness—translate directly into operational friction, staff attrition, and long-term costs in public administration, healthcare, and nonprofit settings.

### Case: Local Government – The Engineer Who Passed the Exam

A county public works engineer aced a classification exam grounded in technical codes and design standards. Promoted to division chief, he immediately inherited a budget, two bargaining units, and a politically sensitive capital program that demanded political judgment, not just technical solutions. Within months, operational friction caused delays to mount and grievances to rise.

The failure was rooted in his success formula (solve technical problems yourself) clashing with the new role (align stakeholders, delegate, sequence trade-offs). Staff confusion over shifting priorities and the leader's inability to navigate union rules exacerbated the backlog, costing the county time and credibility, leading to the predictable payment of managerial tuition.

*Lesson tags*: Technical ≠ leadership; exam blind spots; organizational cost.

### Case: Nonprofit – The Grants Manager Who Became Director

A small, regional arts nonprofit promoted its most successful Grants Manager to Executive Director after she secured two large, multi-year foundation awards. Her technical competence in grant writing, financial compliance, and reporting was unparalleled, making her the "safe" choice to protect the organization's revenue. Once in the director role, she immediately struggled to shift from fiscal oversight to fundraising vision and staff development. She insisted on reviewing and editing every grant application detail herself (micromanagement) and failed to delegate donor cultivation tasks, viewing them as secondary to the technical compliance she mastered.

Within nine months, the staff's senior program officer resigned due to burnout from having their work constantly duplicated and redone. Donor renewals stalled because the new Director could not move beyond reporting on past compliance to articulating a compelling future vision. The organization was technically solvent but functionally paralyzed, paying heavy *managerial tuition* in lost talent and missed growth opportunities.

*Lesson tags:* Technical compliance ≠ strategic vision; reliance on solo heroics inhibits delegation and fundraising

**Case: Healthcare – The Clinical Specialist Turned Supervisor**

In a hospital setting, the top wound-care specialist became a unit manager after scoring highest on a clinical knowledge assessment. While she excelled at protocols, she struggled to deliver effective feedback, reconcile staffing patterns with census trends, and properly steward overtime. Patient metrics remained stable, but staff morale dipped as conflict was suppressed and disengagement set in. The hidden cost was a year of silent disengagement, as staff quickly learned the new manager could not handle the difficult, non-clinical performance conversations required of a leader.

*Lesson tags:* Competence misalignment; delayed support; morale risk.

# Factor 2: Promotion from Within

Promotion from within is a cultural pillar of public service and nonprofit organizations, prized for its ability to preserve institutional memory, signal clear pathways for advancement, and enhance retention. Internal mobility is a critical strategic asset that capitalizes on existing knowledge and mission commitment.

Yet beneath this valuable tradition lies a subtle trade-off. Every organization wants to reward dedication, but when the line between recognition and readiness blurs, longevity can eclipse leadership potential. Many agencies quietly assume that those who have "paid their dues" have also developed the complex, distinct skills required to lead. This untested assumption creates a slow, dangerous drift from merit to seniority—a well-intentioned practice that risks prioritizing familiarity over true capability.

## The Peer-to-Boss Transition

The transition from peer to supervisor is perhaps the most perilous shift in a professional career. The administrator promoted from within must overcome the inherent psychological barrier of leading former colleagues and equals. This demands a massive shift from peer advocacy to managerial accountability.

- **Identity Shift:** New managers struggle precisely because their identity was built around individual contribution and technical mastery, rather than leading through others. They often view delegation as a loss of control and struggle to let go of the technical work they excelled at. Hill (2022) and Ibarra (2015) highlight this shift, noting that former peers who once validated competence may now resist authority, leaving the new leader stranded between two roles—no longer one of the team, not yet trusted by management.
- **Candor Gap:** New internal leaders often struggle with crucial administrative duties like conducting candid performance reviews, managing interpersonal conflict, or simply delegating, due to fear of damaging long-standing relationships or facing resentment from those who were passed over. The pressure to remain "one of the team" inhibits the critical candor required for managerial effectiveness.
- **Need for Scaffolding:** An internal promotion is a success only if the candidate has been deliberately scaffolded for the new role, making them productive on day one and avoiding the costly acclimation period that plagues unprepared external hires. Without this structured support, the expert succeeds only when the system provides a leadership bridge rather than a promotion cliff.

**Case: Local Government – The Senior Analyst**

A city's budget office filled a manager vacancy by elevating the most senior analyst. An expert in spreadsheets and year-end closeouts, she struggled dramatically to set priorities for a team of eight and to negotiate effectively with other departments. Her reliance on technical micromanagement was a visible compensation for a lack of confidence in her new managerial identity. Staff respected her technical knowledge but felt micromanaged, and cross-departmental meetings stalled. Only after a mentorship match with an experienced deputy and a targeted course on influence and conflict did the team stabilize—a costly stabilization lag that resulted from rewarding seniority without readiness.

*Lesson tags:* Seniority ≠ readiness; targeted mentoring; stabilization lag.

### Case: Nonprofit – The Long-Tenured Program Coordinator

A statewide nonprofit promoting food security promoted a 12-year coordinator to program director. While internal morale soared initially, the director immediately ran into the candor gap, avoiding hard performance conversations with two long-time peers, and grant reporting began to slip. The board intervened by introducing stretch assignments (leading a cross-agency working group) and quarterly feedback, directly addressing her reluctance to hold former peers accountable. This intentional scaffolding helped reporting recover and partnerships improve within six months.

*Lesson tags:* Loyalty benefit; candor gap; scaffolding matters.

### Case: Healthcare – The Charge Nurse Who Couldn't Delegate

A large public hospital promoted its most reliable Charge Nurse to Unit Manager of the intensive care unit (ICU). She had 15 years of exceptional clinical competence, navigating every medical crisis with calm and precision, and was rewarded for her reliability. However, she could not manage the peer-to-boss transition with her former colleagues, who were now her direct reports. Instead of delegating staff scheduling and patient load assignments, she continued to personally manage the most complex cases and check every chart, believing her clinical standard was the only safe one.

This refusal to let go resulted in chronic overtime costs and a breakdown of trust with her experienced nursing staff. Within four months, she received two anonymous grievances citing excessive workload and an inability to empower staff. The hospital eventually provided an external executive coach focused specifically on delegation, trust building, and setting performance expectations to mitigate the crisis.

*Lesson tags:* Reliability readiness; inability to shift from doing to leading the work

> **Quick Check: Is Seniority Driving This Promotion?**
>
> Ask these five questions before final selection to ensure readiness is prioritized over mere longevity:
>
> **Evidence**: What concrete, validated behaviors demonstrate the candidate has successfully led *people* through a change or complex project, not merely managed *tasks* to completion?
>
> **Transfer**: Where has the candidate previously navigated significant conflict or resistance from colleagues or stakeholders and still delivered the required results?
>
> **Judgment**: Can the candidate clearly explain a difficult trade-off they have made involving program goals, fiscal constraints, and equity implications, justifying their decision strategically?
>
> **Feedback**: What do peers and direct reports (not just supervisors) say via structured input about the candidate's ability to coach, delegate, and maintain candor?
>
> **Development**: If selected, what is the specific, pre-determined 90-day development plan (mentor assignment, required training, structured check-ins) that will be in place on day one?

## Factor 3: Favoritism and Personal Preference

Not every misaligned promotion is the product of impersonal exams or unexamined seniority. Sometimes, the failure is born of subjective judgment: leaders choose people they like, those who mirror their style, share their networks, or signal personal loyalty—over those who are most objectively qualified. Organizational research labels this **favoritism** or **cronyism**: conferring advantages based on personal relationships rather than competence.

This practice is fundamentally corrosive because, in public service, the perceived fairness of the process is as vital as the competence of the appointee. When relationships supersede merit, the organization exposes itself to severe legal, ethical, and organizational consequences. Favoritism often creates a powerful, self-serving loop: the decision-maker gains an ally, and the appointee gains authority, but the organization and the public lose confidence and competence.

## Ethical and Legal Exposure

Favoritism represents a direct betrayal of the foundational principles of public administration. It violates the mandate of the ASPA Code of Ethics (2013), which requires public administrators to "treat all persons with fairness, justice, and equality and respect individual differences". More practically, it destabilizes credibility because staff perceive leadership selection as patronage reborn, instantly rupturing the sense of a professional, merit-based career service.

The legal jeopardy is clear, particularly within the U.S. context. In federal practice, the legal architecture explicitly guards against favoritism through Merit System Principles and bars specific Prohibited Personnel Practices (PPPs), such as nepotism or granting unauthorized preference. This makes favoritism not just bad policy, but a reportable legal violation handled by the U.S. Merit Systems Protection Board (MSPB). MSPB studies consistently emphasize that perceptions of favoritism erode the integrity of merit systems and damage workforce effectiveness. The ethical damage extends to the duty of care (Chapter 2) because a favored candidate is often promoted based on a personal trust assumption, completely bypassing the preparation necessary for success. This neglect is an ethical failure of stewardship, sacrificing team well-being for personal convenience.

## The Cost of Upward Managing

Favoritism corrodes perceptions of fairness, undermines trust, and invites fundamental performance problems. The organizational mechanism is consistent: where selection feels relational, morale and collaboration suffer dramatically. When employees suspect that performance and fairness are secondary to personal ties, they disengage and the psychological contract is broken.

This dynamic often manifests as the "upward managing" phenomenon, where the favored leader prioritizes pleasing the appointing authority (upward managing) over setting priorities and supporting their team (downward leading).

The costs are multi-layered:

- **Erosion of Candor:** The favored leader is typically reluctant to deliver bad news or contradictory analysis to their patron, creating internal "echo chambers" where dissent and critical feedback cannot rise. This silences critical voices and leads to missed operational risks and long-term failure.
- **Performance Misalignment:** The leader prioritizes activity visible to their patron (e.g., fast communication, political messaging) rather than core operational deliverables (e.g., rigorous fiscal stewardship, delegation, compliance).
- **Talent Attrition:** Competent, non-favored staff recognize the ceiling imposed by the relational selection process. They often respond with cynicism, moral injury, or flight, leading to the turnover of career deputies and high performers—the ultimate payment of *managerial tuition*.

Ethical stewardship requires systems that are strong enough to withstand personal bias, recognizing that the efficiency gained by choosing an "insider" is always dwarfed by the long-term cost of lost integrity and manufactured incompetence. This corruption of the selection process is not confined to one sector, demonstrating that the human urge to choose for comfort and familiarity—rather than for objective readiness—is a universal systemic threat. The following two cases illustrate how selection based on personal preference damages operational performance and public trust in both governmental and non-governmental settings.

## Case: Local Government – The Favored Aide

A newly elected mayor appointed a long-time campaign aide as director of a service department, bypassing a competitive process. The aide excelled at political messaging and relationships with legislative council offices but lacked operational depth. Early political wins successfully secured the appointment, but the operational inadequacy—missed procurement timelines and a spike in contract amendments—caused the turnover of career deputies. The eventual fix required installing a seasoned deputy with explicit authority over operations, which restored balance but left significant reputational scars on the department.

*Lesson tags:* Political alignment ≠ operational readiness; short-term political wins mask long-term operational costs; retention risk; favoritism as a breach of merit.

## Case: Healthcare/Nonprofit – The Like-Minded Manager

A regional health nonprofit's CEO elevated a personable program officer to a cross-functional leadership role after years of volunteer work together. The officer was popular and values-aligned but struggled critically to manage interprofessional tensions with clinicians and data analysts, creating an environment where meetings became echo chambers. Staff cited credibility gaps and a clear pattern of "upward managing" in an external review. The organization later mandated a structured competition for future leadership roles, including a written scenario and peer review panel, to discipline subjective judgment.

*Lesson tags:* Personal comfort over functional fit; "upward managing" creates internal echo chambers; credibility gaps lead to staff cynicism; procedural rigor disciplines bias.

The structural drivers of misalignment—from technical exams that overvalue knowledge (Factor 1), to seniority that substitutes for readiness (Factor 2), to unchecked favoritism that bypasses qualifications (Factor 3)—all lead to the same costly outcome: leaders placed in roles they are unprepared for. Correcting this requires moving beyond criticizing individual leaders and adopting system-level mechanisms that enforce objectivity and transparency in selection. The following tool provides a structured, objective framework for ensuring that promotions are driven by documented readiness, rather than mere availability or personal comfort, acting as a direct countermeasure to the biases identified throughout this chapter.

## Leadership Tool: Competence vs. Readiness Matrix

This four-quadrant tool guides selection conversations, forcing decision-makers to move the focus from technical skill and availability to required growth and development. It is an essential diagnostic framework used to plot candidates or current employees against two distinct and measurable axes: Technical Competence (the ability to *do* the work) and Leadership Readiness (the demonstrated ability to *lead* people, navigate ambiguity, and manage resources). It is used to map candidates against validated leadership competencies (e.g., conflict management, financial stewardship, team building) and technical thresholds, ensuring the promotion process is disciplined, objective, and documented. The required documentation of this mapping helps institutionalize rigor, making it harder to justify a promotion based solely on personal preference or familiarity.

The four quadrants dictate distinct talent management strategies:

- **High Technical / High Leadership Readiness → Promote Now.** This candidate possesses both the deep technical expertise and the demonstrated managerial capacity required for the next level. They have successfully managed conflict, delegated appropriately, and shown strategic thinking, making them a low-risk, high-return appointment ready for immediate empowerment and new responsibility.

- **High Technical / Low Leadership Readiness→Delay + Develop.** This is the classic "promoted into incompetence" risk—the individual excels at the technical work but lacks proven managerial skills or experience. The strategy here is deliberate deceleration: use intensive mentoring, focused stretch assignments, and structured feedback to build readiness *before* promotion, not after, protecting both the individual and the organization from *managerial tuition*.
- **Low Technical / High Leadership Readiness→Consider Role Fit.** This candidate may not have the highest level of technical expertise but demonstrates exceptional leadership behaviors, such as strong emotional intelligence, effective delegation, and coalition building. They could excel in roles that orchestrate work (program coordination, partnerships) where they can manage the process and people, supported by technical advisors who handle specialized details.
- **Low Technical / Low Leadership Readiness→Not Ready.** This individual is a poor fit for a promotion at this time, lacking both the technical foundation and the necessary leadership competencies. The focus must be on clarifying their current role and building fundamental development planning at the individual contributor level before any discussion of upward mobility can begin.

## Conclusion - Putting the Drivers Together (and Looking Ahead)

These three drivers—technical testing that privileges specific skill, internal mobility that defaults to seniority, and favoritism that bypasses qualifications—often coexist, weaving the structural fabric of leadership misalignment. The outcome is the same: organizations elevate skilled doers without adequate preparation and then blame individuals for failures that their own structures have set in motion.

Favoritism, in particular, breaches the ethical duty of care to the individual being promoted and to the team being led. Ethical stewardship requires systems strong enough to withstand personal bias and honor the merit principle not just in letter, but in practice. Collective competence cannot be sustained in a culture where rules are seen as optional for insiders.

## Bridge to Chapter 4

If Part I detailed the **structural drivers** that create misalignment, Part II (Chapter 4) examines the developmental deficits that prevent new leaders from correcting it. The absence of training, the lack of structured mentorship, and the broader de-emphasis of management education don't just fail to fix the problem—they often amplify it by sending newly appointed leaders into complex roles without a map or scaffolding. On the other side of that diagnosis, we will turn to the intentional pipelines and tools that reverse the dynamic and build leaders who are genuinely ready.

# Chapter 4 – Systemic Drivers of Incompetence (Part II)

> We promote people for what they have done, then fault them for what they were never taught to do.

Promotion into leadership is one of the most consequential transitions in any organization. It represents trust, recognition, and opportunity—but it also exposes a recurring flaw in how institutions think about readiness. This flaw is less about the merit principle itself and more about the institutional failure to follow through on the preparation mandate that merit implies. We assume that those who have performed well will automatically lead well, yet the skills that ensure technical success are not the same ones that make leadership effective. The result is predictable: leaders who care deeply and work hard but enter their new roles without the preparation they need to succeed, forcing them to pay *managerial tuition* not through a lack of effort, but a chronic deficit of applicable managerial knowledge. This chapter investigates the systemic decision to under-invest in the leader that the organization has already chosen

## From Structure to Development

In Chapter 3, we examined how structural systems—flawed merit rules, unexamined internal promotion cultures, and subjective favoritism—create the initial conditions that allow leadership misalignment to occur. These are the sins of commission—the deliberate choices that elevate the unprepared. This chapter turns the focus from these structures to the sins of omission—exploring how public, healthcare, and nonprofit organizations unintentionally deepen the problem by failing to prepare the leaders they promote.

This transition marks the intellectual midpoint of the book, shifting our diagnosis from the selection mechanism to the developmental environment. It is not enough to select the right person; the organization must also provide the right path. This principle is a fundamental component of the ethical duty of care that organizations owe to both their employees and the citizens they serve. Two developmental failures stand out as the most damaging omissions in the leadership pipeline: Factor 4 is the pervasive lack of training and mentorship that leaves new supervisors improvising their way through the complex craft of leadership. Factor 5 is the macro-level de-emphasis of public-management education—the shrinking space in higher education where the vital logic of accountability, ethics, and hands-on management is actually taught. Together, they form the readiness gap: the structural and pedagogical distance between technical competence and demonstrated leadership capability.

## Factor 4 - Lack of Training and Mentorship

### The Readiness Gap

Public-sector promotion often assumes that leadership is instinctive. Employees are selected for what they know, not for how they will lead others. Without training or mentorship, they revert to the very behaviors that earned them promotion—solving problems themselves rather than developing the capacity of their teams. Across agencies and nonprofits, the result is consistent: early mistakes in supervision, documentation, budgeting, or conflict management cost far more to fix than it would have cost to prevent them.

This lack of structured development is the precise moment when *managerial tuition* is incurred. Where this pattern plays out differently is in the nature of the costs: In healthcare, the deficit leads to compliance breaches and patient safety risks; in local government, it results in operational backlogs and public trust erosion; and in nonprofits, it quickly risks mission drift and donor confidence.

### Why Training and Competency Initiatives Fail

A growing public-sector literature makes two things clear. First, well-designed leadership development works. In a panel study of a large U.S. federal agency, a multifaceted program that combined coaching, classroom instruction, feedback, and experiential learning measurably improved leader performance and was associated with higher organizational effectiveness where leaders received the intervention. Second, the context of government—goal ambiguity, multiple principals, formalization of HR/budget/procurement—constrains leader discretion, making effective preparation even more essential.

At the same time, public health and allied fields warn that many competency initiatives suffer from fuzzy definitions and weak measurement. In a review of leadership competency sets grounded in Senge's "learning organization" and Burns's "transformational leadership," Reid and Dold (2017) found frequent use of the terms, but rare operational clarity and almost no evidence of implementation fidelity or rigorous assessment (p. 204).

Put bluntly: we talk a lot about competencies, but we don't consistently define, teach, or measure them. The challenge is systemic:

- **Lack of Operational Definitions:** Many key leadership terms (e.g., "systems thinking," "cultural competence") are used often but lack a common, precise definition of the specific knowledge, skills, behaviors, and attitudes associated with them.
- **Measurement Blind Spot:** There is virtually no attention to specifying the standards by which competence should be measured or the means to reliably measure its attainment, especially in action. Relying on self-assessment or passing general examinations is insufficient.

Training programs, therefore, often fail because they provide awareness without a clear pathway to capability. They offer inspiration rather than instruction, leaving the new leader with a certificate but no functional toolkit for the first difficult performance review or budget trade-off.

## The High Return on Investment (ROI) of Public Training

This failure to invest rigorously is compounded by the fact that effective training yields a measurable return, challenging the common misconception that training is a mere expense or a perk.

An econometric study comparing the U.S. and U.K. found that additional episodes of public-employer-provided training were associated with wage gains (a proxy for productivity):

- In the U.S. sample, roughly +6% per episode for public-sector training versus +2% for private-sector training.
- For the United Kingdom, the effects were smaller but still positive: +0.7% for public-sector training versus +0.9% for private-sector training.

The study also observed that public-sector training traveled: private-sector workers benefitted from training they'd received in government, and (in the U.S.) public-sector workers could benefit from prior private-sector training. This portability suggests real skill growth and implies that leadership development is not just a perk; it's a capability investment that follows the person and compounds organizational value over careers. When the public sector invests in robust, structured management training, it increases the collective competence of the overall workforce, regardless of where that talent ultimately works. The cost of training is an up-front investment in systemic performance, while the cost of failure (turnover, rework, audit findings) is a non-recuperable payment of managerial tuition.

Yet Méndez and Sepúlveda (2016) also show that private-sector training is often more selective, while public-sector training shows less evidence of selection on unobserved traits in the U.S. This raises the critical possibility that while who gets trained in government may be more equitable, training is not consistently targeted to readiness or critical role demands, further diluting the ROI.

## The Necessity of Multimodal Development

The evidence points toward a clear solution to the failures of event-based learning: **multimodal intervention**. Multimodal development is a strategic approach that moves beyond single, isolated training events—like a one-day seminar—to integrate multiple, mutually reinforcing methods of learning and support over time. This approach recognizes that complex skills, like leadership, cannot be absorbed passively; they must be developed actively through a blend of formal instruction, relational coaching, experiential practice, and objective feedback. It is a holistic design intended to maximize the transfer of learning from a theoretical concept to actual, observed workplace performance. Where training initiatives fail, the collapse is due to a consistent pattern of isolated, ineffective delivery methods, which include:

- **Event-Based Learning Divorced from Role Transitions:** This occurs when professional development is treated as an isolated event—such as a generic "leadership" seminar or retreat—that is completely unrelated to the actual, high-stakes transition a leader is about to undertake. By separating the learning event from the job context, the organization fails to anchor theory in practice, resulting in high levels of awareness but minimal capability transfer. This approach delivers temporary inspiration instead of functional skills.
- **Mentorship by Happenstance:** In many organizations, mentorship is a resource leaders receive only if they are lucky enough to have a supervisor who is both capable of and dedicated to informal coaching. This lack of intentional structure means the critical transfer of tacit management knowledge (the unwritten rules of negotiation, political context, and interpersonal navigation) is lost for most emerging leaders. When the system institutionalizes learning that relies on luck, the readiness gap widens, leaving new managers "airborne with no instruments".
- **Competency Inflation:** This is the administrative failure of relying on long lists of desirable traits (e.g., "systems thinking," "cultural competence") that lack precise operational definitions and verifiable standards. Without a common, precise definition of the specific knowledge, skills, behaviors, and attitudes associated with competence, the organization cannot consistently teach or measure the trait, rendering the list useless as a developmental guide.
- **No Feedback Loop:** Leadership growth is accelerated by self-awareness and adjustment, but leaders rarely receive structured, multisource feedback tied directly to specific developmental plans. Reliance on unreliable methods, such as self-report or general examinations, perpetuates the Readiness Illusion (Chapter 1) because the absence of objective, multisource data prevents the leader from accurately diagnosing their own blind spots or recognizing when their performance has failed to meet organizational standards.

### Practice Note – Design for Transfer, Not Applause

Programs that blend methods (classroom + coaching + feedback + stretch assignments) outperform stand-alone workshops, particularly in public settings where context constraints are real. Build explicit on-the-job application into the design; require line-manager involvement; and define observable behaviors to verify growth. This approach ensures that the learning is transferred from the classroom to the crucial moment of application in the workplace.

## Case Illustrations: The Cost of Untaught Management

The organizational commitment to one-dimensional, event-based training produces failures that are both systematic and entirely preventable. The isolation of training from job reality, the absence of mentorship, the vagueness of competency frameworks, and the lack of a structured feedback loop (the four consistent failure modes) all combine to guarantee that new leaders, regardless of their intrinsic talent, are functionally unprepared. This neglect constitutes a systemic breach of the *ethical duty of care* to the emerging leader, forcing them to learn crucial managerial skills—such as conflict documentation, fiscal oversight, and delegation—in real-time, high-stakes environments.

When organizations under-invest in this *multimodal development*, good employees inevitably stumble into avoidable administrative failures. The following three cases, drawn from public, healthcare, and nonprofit sectors, illustrate the predictable translation of developmental deficits into operational friction, staff attrition, and the non-recuperable payment of *managerial tuition*. These are not stories of individual weakness, but of institutional omission.

## Case (Local Government)

A county parks department implemented a structured mentorship program after a string of minor compliance issues in its maintenance division. Under the new approach, every newly promoted crew leader was paired with a mentor dyad—one senior field supervisor and one operations analyst. The mentors guided each new leader through a

90-day onboarding plan: reviewing procurement rules, approving work orders in the finance system, and conducting a weekly walk-through focused on safety and documentation. One recent promotee, a grounds-equipment specialist, admitted he had never completed a budget variance form or entered an accident report before his promotion. By week 6, he could explain the county's purchasing thresholds, spot incomplete timesheets, and lead a five-minute safety huddle without notes. Within a year, incident reports dropped by 20 percent and project close-outs improved.

*The lesson* was clear: mentorship institutionalized learning that used to depend on luck—and prevented good employees from stumbling into avoidable administrative failures.

## Case (Healthcare)

A regional hospital network launched an internal "Leadership Academy" to prepare emerging nurse managers and clinical supervisors. The inaugural cohort completed a two-day retreat on communication and change management, followed by monthly webinars. Initial evaluations glowed—participants valued the content and certificates—but unit-level indicators hardly budged. Six months later, a redesign paired each participant with a mentorship dyad (one clinical mentor and one administrative mentor) and added a required 90-day improvement sprint drawn from each unit's safety or efficiency priorities. The difference was measurable: turnover among new supervisors fell by eight percent, self-reported engagement climbed, and incident-report closure times improved.

*The lesson* was clear—formal training inspires awareness, but integrated learning with mentorship, feedback, and practical accountability changes performance.

**Case (Nonprofit)**

A mid-sized human-services nonprofit hired a policy analyst as program director based on her stellar evaluation portfolio. She inherited 30 staff, a braided funding model (a program financed by several grants and contracts with distinct reporting rules), and complex performance requirements. The first quarter brought late submissions, staff churn, and a funder warning. The turning point came only after the board approved a management mini curriculum (supervision fundamentals, budget variance analysis, outcome reporting) paired with executive coaching and a stakeholder mapping project.

*The lesson* mirrored this chapter: analysis ≠ leadership; without management education and guided practice, promotions become stress tests

## Factor 5 – De-Emphasis of Public-Management Education

Leadership readiness begins before the first supervisory role—it often starts with the intellectual framework provided by graduate education. But in many corners of the academy, the balance has shifted: policy analysis and technical specialization receive pride of place; management preparation—supervision, budgeting, ethics, performance management—gets less sustained attention. This trend is dangerous because it means the next generation of public servants are being equipped with high-level analytic skills but lack the process-level competence required for day-to-day organizational execution

### The Structural Drift to "Why" Over "How"

This shift reflects a structural drift in higher education. A national analysis of political science–housed public administration programs in the United States found empirical evidence of this trend, concluding that the core attention within both government and higher education is increasingly focused on politics and policies rather than on management (Braga, 2020, p. 284).

> **Quantitative Evidence of Drift:** Braga (2020) demonstrated this decline in status within political science departments by revealing key metrics: the proportion of public administration degrees fell from 33.8% (2006) to 26.7% (2016) within those departments. Crucially, the percentage of programs offering advanced methods within public administration

dropped by a staggering 47.3% (from 16.9% to 8.9%) over the same decade. Public administration programs themselves are highly concentrated at the master's level (68.5% of programs are master's), suggesting it is viewed as a narrow professional specialization rather than a foundational discipline, further reinforcing its distance from core university research agendas (Braga, 2020, p. 288).

These indicators point to a structural drift: if the educational center of gravity privileges policy theory and quantitative analysis untethered to managerial practice, graduates may arrive with strong analytic skills but thin preparation for the first roles where success hinges on people leadership, fiscal stewardship, and ethical judgment.

As former Federal Reserve Chairman Paul Volcker famously noted, when prospective civil servants attend schools of public policy, they are often learning how to debate political issues, not "how to run the goddamn government" (Sorkin, 2018). This imbalance creates a profound threat: the education system trains students with advanced knowledge on **why** governments exist but offers limited awareness on **how** public sector organizations actually operate —including the logic, tools, and systems that govern accountability and service delivery. This structural gap is what agencies are then forced to address through reactive, on-the-job training, often too late to prevent initial leadership failures.

## The Managerial Skills Deficit and "Wicked Problems"

The focus on policy analysis is vital for developing critical thinkers, but it often sacrifices the teaching of the management craft. This creates a critical deficit in the essential process, people, and performance skills required for first-line leadership. This deficit is manageable when dealing with straightforward, technical issues (sometimes called "tame problems"), but it becomes catastrophic when leaders encounter the kind of complex, systemic challenges that define modern public service.

Furthermore, the complexity of modern challenges demands managers who can handle not just technical problems, but **"wicked problems"**—social and organizational issues that resist traditional linear, analytical approaches. Coined by Rittel and Webber (1973), these are planning and policy dilemmas—such as homelessness, climate change adaptation, or deep-seated public health crises—that are characterized by having no clear solution, no definitive stopping point, and shifting requirements. The analytic skills prized in policy school are insufficient for managing these realities, which are instead defined by ambiguity, stakeholder conflict, and constant uncertainty.

These "wicked problems" require managers to blend policy knowledge with practical collaboration, negotiation, and the intellectual necessity of cross-contamination with other humanistic disciplines. This means a manager must be equipped to engage with ethics, sociology, and democracy as fluid managerial tools, rather than just abstract theories. When graduate programs do not explicitly teach these adaptive and relational skills, they are producing analysts who are intellectually prepared for the *logic* of the problem but fundamentally unprepared to face the unstructured, politically charged reality of public sector work. The lack of preparation for these complex realities—which are endemic in public and nonprofit sectors—is often what breaks the newly promoted leader, quickly transforming policy ambition into organizational paralysis.

## Why This Matters for Readiness and Equity

The structural drift in academia—where policy analysis overshadows the management craft—has profound consequences for both the operational capacity and the ethical mandate of public organizations. The de-emphasis of public management education creates a critical vacuum for practitioners, forcing them to learn vital, high-stakes leadership skills in crisis rather than preparation. This failure is particularly acute for emerging supervisors because the required managerial skills are treated as "soft" or optional, leading to a predictable breakdown of both team morale and public accountability. Furthermore, the lack of formal, structured learning routes for management skills exacerbates existing systemic inequities. The consequences of this deficit are evident on several fronts:

- **First-line management is practice-heavy.** New supervisors need essential skills in running a meeting, setting standards, managing conflict, coaching, and documenting decisions in compliant ways. When these are treated as "on-the-job learnings," failure becomes *managerial tuition* paid not just by the leader, but by their teams and the communities they serve.
- **Education influences organizational investment.** If graduate curricula signal that leadership is a "soft" skill secondary to quantitative analysis, agencies may follow suit by over-weighting technical credentials in hiring and under-weighting early investment in mentored transitions. This perpetuates the cycle of *manufactured incompetence* by prioritizing yesterday's technical success over tomorrow's leadership demands.
- **Equity implications.** When leadership is learned informally, access to *tacit knowledge*—the unwritten rules of negotiation, political context, and network access—flows primarily through privileged networks and sponsorship. Formal education that centers public management (not just policy) can counteract that inequity by providing a structured, meritocratic pathway to acquiring managerial skills, leveling the playing field for emerging leaders by demystifying the management craft and making it accessible to all.

**A brief international note:** Workforce development patterns differ by country. In comparative panel data, public employees generally receive more training on average than private employees, and training participation is higher in the U.K. than the U.S. (Méndez & Sepúlveda, 2016). While this is about employer training, it suggests institutional context shapes the supply of development—and that U.S. agencies must lean harder into structured management preparation if higher education continues to tilt toward policy analysis.

**Quick Check – Audit Your Pipeline**

Ask these pointed questions to reveal your organization's hidden assumptions about leadership development:

- Where do your hires learn supervision, budgeting, and ethics—in school or only on the job?
- Does your tuition reimbursement or professional development nudge toward courses with management practice content?
- Do your internships/fellowships include deliverables that demonstrate management behaviors (not just policy memos)?

**Leadership Tool – Curriculum-to-Practice Bridge (for HR, L&D, and University Partners)**

Bridging the academic-practice divide requires intentional partnership:

- Map critical first-line competencies (people, fiscal, risk, service) to specific course modules in local MPA/MPH/MNP programs.
- Offer capstone residencies in your agency where students lead a small improvement sprint (with mentoring and feedback).
- Build an adjunct pathway for seasoned managers to co-teach supervision and budgeting labs, injecting real-world context into the curriculum.

These interventions—from self-auditing your training assumptions to building genuine academic partnerships—address the critical deficit of management knowledge created by Factor 5. However, the failures in leadership readiness are rarely rooted in a single cause; they are a cumulative organizational liability. The structural problems identified in Chapter 3 are simply magnified by the developmental neglect detailed here. Addressing the crisis of manufactured incompetence therefore demands a comprehensive, integrated strategy that corrects flaws across the entire system, from selection criteria to educational support. The following table summarizes this integrated diagnostic framework, linking the systemic drivers, their resulting developmental failures, and the necessary organizational remedies.

# Systemic Drivers → Developmental Failures → Remedies

The table below summarizes the relationship between the systemic factors (Chapter 3), the developmental failures (Chapter 4), and the solutions presented in the rest of the book.

*Table 4.1 – Systemic Drivers & Remedies*

| Systemic Driver | Developmental Failure | Remedy / Intervention |
|---|---|---|
| Merit and promotion systems prioritize technical tests and seniority. | Leaders elevated without readiness; reliance on technical mastery over leadership capacity. | Introduce blended training, structured onboarding, and competency-based selection tools. |
| Lack of structured mentorship or coaching culture. | New leaders improvise; early errors multiply; morale and compliance suffer. | Institutionalize mentorship dyads, 90-day onboarding plans, and feedback cycles. |
| De-emphasis of management education in universities. | Graduates arrive analytic but unprepared for supervision, budgeting, or ethics. | Strengthen academic-practice partnerships; embed management curricula and residencies. |
| Cultural undervaluing of leadership development. | Leadership viewed as innate or secondary to technical skill. | Reframe development as ethical stewardship; fund leadership pipelines as infrastructure. |

# Conclusion: From Diagnosis to Design

These drivers are mutually reinforcing. When graduate programs under-emphasize public management, organizations that also under-invest in structured training, mentorship, and feedback set new leaders up for the **confidence-competence gap** described in Chapter 1. The outcome is predictable: good "doers" with thin preparation for people leadership.

The evidence base is clear enough to act: multimodal development improves leader and organizational outcomes in government settings; competency frameworks must be defined and measured; and the education-practice bridge needs deliberate construction. Preparation is not optional; it is an ethical imperative and a core function of public stewardship.

## How This Links Back—and Forward

**Back to Chapter 3:** When merit systems and promotion-from-within processes meet the chronic development gaps outlined here, leaders are chosen without an accompanying development runway—effectively manufacturing failure.

**Ahead to Chapter 5:** We now turn from developmental deficits to proactive design. Chapter 5 details the core distinction between technical excellence and leadership competence, providing a practical checklist of leadership competencies and defining the intellectual foundation necessary for building intentional pipelines.

# Chapter 5 – Technical Excellence ≠ Leadership Competence: Bridging the Readiness Gap

*Readiness is the bridge between what leaders know and what their organizations need them to become.*

## The Paradox of Promotion

Promotion into leadership is among the most celebrated transitions in public service—and the least prepared for. The earlier chapters revealed how structural (Chapter 3) and developmental (Chapter 4) systems elevate people for what they have done rather than for what they are ready to do. The paradox is deceptively simple: organizations reward mastery of a task, then demand mastery of people, purpose, and systems without teaching any of it. Technical excellence becomes the passport to a new role whose requirements are entirely different.

Having spent four chapters diagnosing the systemic and developmental failures, we now shift our focus to the individual leader and the nature of the competence they must acquire. The failures of the *system* (unexamined merit rules) and the *institution* (lack of training) manifest as an immediate crisis of *readiness* for the person promoted. The core issue is no longer structural but cognitive and behavioral: the individual must redefine success. In practical terms, this means that highly skilled professionals—analysts, nurses, engineers, planners, accountants—find themselves promoted into jobs defined less by doing and more by enabling. The competencies that once made them indispensable now limit them, and many discover that their old success formula has expired.

In practical terms, this means that highly skilled professionals—analysts, nurses, engineers, planners, accountants—find themselves promoted into jobs defined less by doing and more by enabling. The shift can be jarring. The competencies that once made them indispensable now limit them, and many discover that their old success formula has expired. The human cost of this failure to distinguish between technical skill and managerial readiness becomes immediately apparent in the daily operations of teams across the public sector.

**Case – The Expert Analyst Turned Manager**

A senior analyst in a county finance department was promoted after years of exemplary technical performance. Her reports were flawless, her audits precise, her reputation spotless. Within six months as a section manager, she was exhausted. Staff morale had collapsed, and turnover doubled. Her instinct was to fix problems herself, not to coach others to solve them. For instance, she spent an entire week re-checking an audit of less importance, causing her to miss two strategic deadlines for the department head. "I can't rely on them," she explained. Her mentor responded gently, "They'll never learn if you keep doing their work". Her story is common: technical excellence rewarded, leadership readiness assumed. The organizational cost here—wasted time, two high-priority deadlines missed, and doubled turnover—is a direct consequence of a promotion system that ignored the risk of misaligned competence (Chapter 2).

Unlike the engineer in Chapter 3 who struggled with supervision in public works, this analyst's challenge was cognitive rather than procedural—a failure to shift from precision to prioritization. Together, the two cases illustrate how misalignment takes many forms across technical domains.

*Lesson tags*: Technical mastery managerial competence; failure to shift from precision to prioritization; micromanagement as a failure of delegation and trust; misaligned competence leads directly to measurable turnover and managerial tuition.

## From Expert to Leader: The Identity Shift

The transition from expert to leader is fundamentally one of identity dissonance. Individuals who once measured their worth by personal output and technical competence must now succeed through the competence and growth of others. Technical competence is a relationship with *things* (data, code, budgets); leadership competence is a relationship with *people* (motivation, conflict, culture). This demands not just a cognitive shift in priorities, but a profound emotional and psychological adjustment. Experts rely on certainty, precision, and control—qualities that can hinder adaptive leadership. Leaders, by contrast, must learn to tolerate ambiguity, delegate imperfectly, and find satisfaction in the growth of a team rather than the polish of their own work.

Linda Hill's (1992) seminal research on new managers described this difficulty vividly: the new role is characterized by interdependence and managing a demanding web of relationships, not just tasks. William Bridges (2009) adds that all true transitions contain a "neutral zone," a disorienting period where the old professional identity fades before the new one fully takes hold. Herminia Ibarra (2015) calls the required change "acting into leadership," noting that growth often happens by experimenting with new behaviors until they feel authentic, rather than waiting to feel ready. That ambiguity, however disorienting, is precisely where effective leadership begins. The ability to successfully navigate this transition defines the difference between a high-performing individual contributor and a high-performing manager

## The Learning Loop of Competence

Leadership competence is not innate, but rather learned through an iterative process of assessment, challenge, and support. Day and Dragoni (2015) describe this development as a continuous cycle or learning loop. The emerging leader must first be assessed (to identify the gap), given a challenging stretch assignment (to apply new behaviors), and then provided with support (mentorship and structured feedback) to integrate the learning. Without all three components, the loop breaks, and the new leader defaults to old, comfortable behaviors. This necessity for experiential, supported learning reinforces the need for multimodal development (Chapter 4), where theory and practice intertwine to build competence in real time.

The necessity of the learning loop—combining assessment, challenge, and support—demands that the emerging leader first achieve radical self-awareness. Before any organization can intervene with training or mentorship, the individual must pause to audit their own behaviors and identify where the old success formula is still hindering them. The following quick check forces this immediate confrontation with the distinction between doing and leading.

> **Quick Check – Are You Leading or Doing?**
>
> - Do you measure success by what you accomplish or by what your team achieves?
> - How often do you solve problems your staff could handle?
> - When was the last time you taught someone a skill you once guarded?

Moving from this essential moment of self-reflection, the organization and the individual need a common language to define the required skills. Competence in leadership is not merely a philosophical attitude; it is a measurable, behavioral set of capabilities that must be explicitly taught and assessed.

## Core Competencies of Leadership Readiness

Competence in leadership is observable and teachable. It moves beyond technical skill toward a distinct set of relational, strategic, and systemic capabilities. Boyatzis (2018) and Spencer and Spencer (1993) identify behavioral indicators that distinguish effective leaders from technical experts, such as emotional intelligence, communication, delegation, and ethical decision-making. The U.S. Office of Personnel Management's **Executive Core Qualifications (ECQs)** offer a proven, public-sector framework, grouping necessary skills into five key clusters—*Leading Change, Leading People, Results Driven, Business Acumen,* and *Building Coalitions*—providing a shared language for defining readiness.

### Competence-to-Readiness Matrix

The difference between technical expertise and leadership competence is not stylistic; it is functional. Technical experts reduce variation. Leaders manage meaning. They translate vision into priorities and cultivate competence in others. The table below illustrates the critical functional divergence:

*Table 5.1 – Functional Divergence: Technical Excellence vs. Leadership Competence*

| Dimension | Technical Excellence | Leadership Competence |
|---|---|---|
| Focus | Accuracy and execution | Direction and influence |
| Time Horizon | Immediate deliverables | Long-term outcomes |
| Measure of Success | Personal output | Team capacity and results |
| Primary Skill | Analysis and precision | Communication and vision |
| Key Risk | Perfectionism and over-control | Delegation and trust |

## The Non-Negotiable Core: Emotional Intelligence

The most critical functional divergence lies in **Emotional Intelligence (EQ)**. Daniel Goleman's (1998) work reinforces this distinction: leaders with high self-awareness, empathy, and social skill outperform those who rely solely on intellect or technical mastery. Leadership competence is therefore relational—it depends on how effectively one mobilizes others toward shared goals.

For the newly promoted expert, this shift is often the most disorienting, as the metrics for success move from binary (right/wrong) to nuanced (influence/trust). The precision that defined technical excellence must be supplemented by the adaptive capability to manage human variables, making EQ the non-negotiable floor for effective leadership in complex public, healthcare, and nonprofit environments.

Boyatzis (2018) identifies behavioral indicators that distinguish effective leaders from technical experts, grouping EQ into three key clusters essential for the public, healthcare, and nonprofit environments:

- **Cognitive Competencies:** These relate to pattern recognition and include systems thinking and pattern analysis—the ability to see the connections between policy, resources, and public outcomes. This competence enables leaders to understand that local operational failures often stem from upstream systemic drivers (Chapter 3) and to apply holistic, rather than piece-meal, solutions to complex organizational challenges.
- **Emotional Competencies:** These focus on self-management and include emotional self-control and adaptability—the capacity to remain calm and focused during crisis and political pressure. For leaders in public service, this cluster is vital for withstanding the intense scrutiny and inherent conflict that arises when pursuing adaptive work (Chapter 9), ensuring the leader's emotional state does not drive organizational instability.
- **Social Competencies:** These relate to relationship management and include empathy and organizational awareness—the ability to provide candid feedback and navigate interdepartmental politics without damaging trust. This outward-facing intelligence allows leaders to build effective coalitions (ECQ: *Building Coalitions*) and manage up, down, and across organizational boundaries with integrity and influence.

This distinction proves that leadership requires a mastery of human dynamics entirely separate from technical mastery. To succeed, the emerging manager must develop the capacity to operate effectively at both the technical and relational levels.

## Developing the "Long-Distance Muscles"

This relational capacity requires specific "long-distance muscles"—the durable competencies that sustain leadership over time and distance. These are the skills that enable a leader to multiply their impact through others, rather than limiting it to their individual output. Developing these muscles is the focus of structured pipeline work (Chapter 6) and intentional developmental support (Chapter 4). The core operational competencies necessary for this relational success include:

- **Vision and Strategic Thinking:** The technical expert views the budget as a compliance document—a ledger to be balanced with accuracy. The leader sees it as a strategic statement that connects organizational values (Chapter 9) to long-term outcomes (ECQ: *Leading Change*), using fiscal data to justify mission choices. Strategic vision demands the ability to conceptualize complex challenges, communicate them clearly, and motivate a team toward an outcome that is not immediately visible.
- **Emotional Intelligence (EQ):** Beyond mere self-awareness, EQ provides the essential skills for delegation, managing conflict, and providing candid performance feedback. These skills are often the first to fail in technically focused leaders who were promoted for their precision, not their ability to handle complexity and emotion. A deficit in EQ leads directly to the breakdown of the psychological contract (Chapter 2) and the proliferation of micromanagement.
- **Fiscal Stewardship and Decision Accountability:** The expert's view of *Business Acumen* (ECQ) stops at accuracy—ensuring the numbers are correct. The leader's view extends to strategic risk management, using fiscal data to justify mission choices, manage procurement, and maintain robust internal controls. This accountability is an ethical duty to protect public resources and manage operational risk proactively.
- **Team Development and Delegation:** This is the leader's primary mechanism for multiplying capacity and avoiding the technical excellence trap. Delegation demands the emotional intelligence to tolerate imperfection, the communication skill to set clear guardrails, and the accountability structure to track progress (ECQ: *Leading People*). The leader must find professional satisfaction in the competence of their team, not in their personal command over tasks.

The functional divergence detailed above demonstrates that leadership competence is a unified craft, not a collection of optional traits. When these "long-distance muscles"—combining relational intelligence, strategic vision, and fiscal accountability—are underdeveloped, the leader does not simply underperform; they actively create systemic drag on the organization. The deficiency translates instantly into operational friction, political exposure, and a costly erosion of team capacity. This is the organizational reality of misaligned competence, which, as the next section explores, carries immediate and measurable costs across every sector.

## Organizational Implications: The Hidden Costs of Misaligned Competence

The functional divergence detailed above demonstrates that leadership competence is a unified craft, not a collection of optional traits. When these "long-distance muscles"—combining relational intelligence, strategic vision, and fiscal accountability—are underdeveloped, the leader does not simply underperform; they actively create systemic drag on the organization. The deficiency translates instantly into operational friction, political exposure, and a costly erosion of team capacity. This is the organizational reality of misaligned competence, which, as the next section explores, carries immediate and measurable costs across every sector.

Misaligned leadership often turns a promotion into an organizational bottleneck, severely impacting the workforce and the public mission. The failure to execute basic managerial functions—delegation, conflict management, and resource stewardship—transforms the leader from a multiplying asset into a consuming liability. This phenomenon creates predictable organizational damage across several vectors:

- **Leadership Drainers:** Untrained managers who prioritize their own control and output become leadership drainers, consuming time and energy by micromanaging, resulting in the documented costs of turnover and low engagement (Chapter 2). Annual data compiled by the American Productivity and Quality Center (APQC) consistently links manager quality directly to employee retention and output. A significant portion of this attrition—the engine of managerial tuition—is attributable to supervisors who lack basic competency in conflict management, coaching, and delegation.

- **Stakeholder Failure:** Competence also requires managing upward (aligning with political or appointed leadership) and outward (aligning with citizens and partners). Gabarro and Kotter (2005) remind us that stakeholder alignment is a measurable leadership competency, and failure here exposes the organization to political and reputational risk. The upward managing behavior often associated with favoritism (Chapter 3) is a prime example of this failure.
- **The Cultural Cost:** These failures are not character flaws. They are systemic results of the untested assumption that people who perform brilliantly at one level will automatically thrive at another. The financial cost is measurable; the cultural cost—the erosion of internal confidence in the system—is harder to repair. When staff realize that promotion is a lottery based on past technical performance, the internal drive for collective competence decays into cynicism.

The translation of these systemic organizational risks into tangible results depends entirely on the structured support provided to the newly promoted manager. The following case illustrates the profound recovery possible when developmental structure is intentionally introduced to correct misaligned competence.

### Case – The Healthcare Supervisor Who Learned to Let Go

A hospital promoted a highly skilled physical therapist to team lead. Initially, she tried to see every patient and supervise staff simultaneously. Her mentor introduced weekly delegation goals—each week she was required to assign more responsibility to others. Within six months, throughput increased 20 percent, and staff satisfaction rose sharply. Her success came not from doing more, but from letting go. As the healthcare example in Chapter 4 demonstrated, developmental neglect often leaves new leaders improvising.

In contrast, this case shows what happens when mentorship and structure are intentionally built into the promotion process. Where Chapter 4's vignette revealed failure born of unpreparedness, this one illustrates recovery through guided readiness—a concrete demonstration that leadership competence can be cultivated, not assumed.

*Lesson tags:* Technical mastery limits scalability; success achieved by delegating authority (not just tasks); structured mentorship accelerates the necessary identity shift; recovery through guided readiness demonstrates competence is cultivatable.

## Building the Bridge: From Awareness to Action

The goal is to bridge the readiness gap by moving from awareness (diagnosis) to intentional action (design). Leadership development is a continuous, experiential process (Day & Dragoni, 2015). Raelin (2016) calls this "work-based learning," where reflection and action intertwine, allowing leaders to develop skills in real time. Structured mentorship accelerates this process by giving emerging leaders safe spaces to practice new behaviors (Allen & Eby, 2010).

Organizations can operationalize these insights by embedding competency development into selection, training, and feedback systems. Ingraham and Getha-Taylor (2005) warn that theory often outpaces practice; bridging this divide requires treating leadership readiness as a strategic asset, not an HR accessory. State and local programs that align training to clearly defined competencies show the strongest performance gains (Getha-Taylor et al., 2011).

## Ethical Reflection: The Duty to Prepare

Public organizations have an ethical responsibility to equip those they promote. Denhardt et al. (2013) describe leadership as stewardship—a duty to serve the public interest through competence and integrity. Neglecting preparation violates that duty. The distinction between doing and leading is a matter of stewardship. When a leader micromanages, it is a failure of trust and delegation, violating the ethical duty of care established in Chapter 9. The failure to invest in readiness is an act of institutional negligence because it guarantees failure and damages the public trust that organizations steward (Chapter 2).

> **Quick Reflection – The Ethics of Readiness**
>
> Think about the last time someone in your organization was promoted. What was done to ensure they were ready? What was assumed?
>
> Promoting without preparation is not simply inefficient—it is ethically negligent. To lead others responsibly, institutions must invest in competence before authority is granted.

## Leadership Tool - Building Competence Pipelines

The commitment to readiness must be formalized through tangible tools and policies that discipline institutional decisions and move beyond subjective judgment. The competency framework established in this chapter is the intellectual engine that drives the actionable tools in Appendix C. Strategic talent management requires action well before the promotion decision:

- **Define measurable leadership competencies before selection.** These must be distinct from technical requirements (e.g., *negotiation skill* vs. *auditing protocol*) and tied directly to organizational outcomes and the ECQ framework.
- **Provide structured "stretch" roles and peer mentoring.** This systemic action corrects the **seniority trap** by testing readiness in low-stakes environments outside of tenure and formal authority.
- **Evaluate readiness with both self- and supervisor assessments.** Utilizing multi-source feedback (like 360-degree

instruments) introduces objective reality to the assessment process, helping to pierce the **Readiness Illusion.**
- **Treat leadership development as a recurring investment, not a remedial expense.** Funding development intentionally prevents the crisis of **managerial tuition** and signals an organizational commitment to **ethical stewardship.**

Implementing these four actions transforms the recruitment and promotion process from a reactive, high-risk reward system into a proactive, intentional pipeline focused on mitigating managerial failure. This structural commitment to readiness is the highest expression of organizational integrity, translating the ethical mandate of stewardship into daily operational policy.

## Conclusion: From Diagnosis to Design

Technical excellence is the foundation on which leadership should be built, not the ceiling that confines it. The distinction between doing and leading is not a matter of preference but of purpose. Bridging that gap requires systems that identify, cultivate, and measure the competencies that turn expertise into effective leadership. The Leadership Alignment Project (Appendix B) is designed precisely for this purpose, providing the experiential framework to apply these concepts.

The systematic failure to define and develop leadership competence requires a focused, intentional organizational response. This response is the subject of the next chapter, which moves from defining *what* competence is, to designing how organizations can intentionally build leadership pipelines, embed structured support, and institutionalize readiness to ensure that promotions lead to sustainable success, not systemic failure.

The next chapter moves from defining those competencies to designing the intentional pipelines that sustain them.

# Chapter 6 - Building Leadership Pipelines with Intention

*Systems, not slogans, sustain leadership readiness.*

The systemic drivers of incompetence (Chapters 3 and 4) prove that when we ignore institutional design, we manufacture failure. This chapter moves from diagnosis to solution: detailing how organizations must stop treating leadership development as a random event and start managing it as essential organizational infrastructure. This chapter translates the readiness gap identified in Chapter 5 into an organizational system for sustained capacity.

## From Individuals to Infrastructure

Every organization praises the idea of "growing our own leaders," yet few actually design the machinery to do it. Too often, leadership development is treated as an event—an occasional workshop, a mentoring pair-up, or an after-action retreat—rather than as an ongoing system that identifies, equips, and sustains leaders over time. When development is episodic, readiness remains accidental. When it becomes infrastructure, readiness becomes predictable.

A leadership pipeline is that infrastructure. It is the deliberate architecture that moves potential leaders from technical mastery to supervisory confidence to strategic stewardship. The fundamental shift here is philosophical:

- **Succession planning focuses on replacement—asking, "Who will fill this seat when it opens?"**. This approach is reactive and seat-centric, treating the leadership role as a siloed vacancy that must be backfilled based on the availability of the best internal candidate. It often defaults to assessing retrospective performance or seniority (Chapter 3), creating the high-risk scenario of promoting competence out of itself. Succession planning is necessary for continuity of authority, but it is insufficient for continuity of capability.

- **Pipeline thinking focuses on capability continuity—asking, "What capabilities must endure regardless of who sits here?".** This approach is proactive and system-centric, recognizing that the long-term health of the organization depends on the perpetual supply of skills—such as fiscal stewardship, strategic thinking, and ethical governance (Chapter 5)—not just names on an organizational chart. This philosophical commitment turns talent management into an infrastructure challenge, viewing competence as an organizational asset to be protected.

Pipelines operate under the belief that competence is a renewable resource that must be tracked and sustained, just like budgets, safety, or compliance. The question is never *whether* leaders will leave; it is *whether* capability will. Organizations that fail to institutionalize leadership view competence as a personnel problem; those that build pipelines view it as a managed asset class. This philosophical distinction is the only effective defense against the systemic risks detailed in Chapters 3 and 4, which otherwise reward short-term technical output while failing to secure long-term capacity. Managing competence as an asset explicitly links talent management to organizational risk management (Chapter 2), ensuring sustained ethical stewardship and mission delivery.

> **Practice Note — Leadership Continuity vs. Succession**
>
> **Leadership continuity** is capacity management; succession fills vacancies. Organizations must consciously shift their focus from the question of who will replace a departing leader to what fundamental organizational capabilities must endure.
>
> **Succession** is a reactive process that fills an immediate seat, often relying on retrospective performance metrics and increasing the risk of misaligned competence. Pipeline thinking, by contrast, views continuity as a predictive system that builds skill depth, tests readiness through experiential learning, and ensures that essential capacity exists before a crisis occurs, allowing the organization to reliably fill futures.

The shift from reactive succession to proactive continuity, which the Practice Note emphasizes, demands a formal operational structure. This structure must translate the philosophical commitment to capability continuity into measurable, sustainable processes that touch every stage of a leader's career. When organizations refuse to rely on luck, they must intentionally design the pipeline's internal architecture to ensure that the development (Chapter 4) and competence (Chapter 5) are tracked, supported, and renewed.

## Anatomy of a Leadership Pipeline

A robust pipeline is modeled not on a linear chart, but on the flow of energy and materials through a system. Every effective pipeline has four working chambers: **identification**, **preparation**, **transition support**, and **renewal**. Each chamber performs a vital function; together they create an upward flow of competence rather than a single, high-stakes promotion gate.

*Table 6.1 — Leadership Pipeline*

| Pipeline Component | Purpose | Illustration |
|---|---|---|
| Identification | Detect emerging leaders early through behavioral signals—initiative, influence, and learning agility. | A city's Public Works department uses project-lead rotations and 360° feedback to spot supervisors who coach effectively. |
| Preparation | Provide structured development before promotion: leadership labs, job shadowing, and project leadership. | A hospital's Charge-to-Manager bridge program trains nurses in budgeting, HR, and change management six months before eligibility. |
| Transition Support | Surround new leaders with mentoring, feedback, and workload buffers during the first 90–180 days. | A nonprofit pairs every new director with a board-appointed mentor and peer learning circle. |
| Retention & Renewal | Keep leadership energy fresh through rotation, advanced study, or sabbaticals. | A state agency offers rotational fellowships every four years to prevent stagnation and broaden perspective. |

The science behind these elements is well established. Day and Dragoni (2015) link leadership effectiveness to deliberate practice and continuous feedback. Raelin (2016) shows that reflection-in-action embeds learning more deeply than classroom exposure alone. Getha-Taylor et al. (2011) demonstrate that competency-based programs in state and local government measurably improve managerial capacity. Pipelines work because they replace chance with design.

The **Identification** chamber is the first line of defense against the systemic flaws of *merit and favoritism* (Chapter 3). Its core function is to systematically detect emerging leaders through observable behavioral signals—initiative, influence, and learning agility—rather than relying solely on retrospective metrics like technical test scores or seniority. This chamber actively corrects the bias toward retrospective performance by insisting on multiple data points, such as the 360-degree feedback mentioned in the illustration, that gauge *prospective capability*. This ensures that talent surfacing is objective, disciplined, and mitigates the tendency to select based on unchecked favoritism or personal trust.

The **Preparation** chamber provides the foundational developmental support, designed to build competence *before* authority is granted. This chamber directly executes the *multimodal development* mandate (Chapter 4), ensuring that the shift to leadership is supported by a blended curriculum of formal classroom training, job shadowing, and essential experiential learning. Programs designed within this chamber, such as hospital charge-to-manager bridge curricula, intentionally expose emerging leaders to core non-technical domains—like budgeting, HR administration, and change management—which are prerequisites for success at the supervisory level.

The **Transition Support** chamber provides the critical scaffolding necessary for the leader's first 90 to 180 days in role. It is the necessary corrective to the *lack of training and mentorship* (Chapter 4), providing the structural assurance that the new leader is not set up for failure. This support typically includes pairing the new manager with a mentor dyad, implementing workload buffers, and enforcing regular coaching sessions focused on difficult conversations and strategic delegation. This critical support prevents the initial errors that often lead to the devastating payment of *managerial tuition* during the first six months.

Finally, the **Retention and Renewal** chamber ensures the pipeline maintains its vitality and prevents the stagnation of tenured staff. This component addresses the strategic necessity of continuous learning, recognizing that even established leaders require new challenges to adapt to evolving organizational and political complexity. Mechanisms like rotational fellowships, advanced study, and planned sabbaticals inject new perspectives into the organization, broadening the experiential base of leadership and ensuring that competence is sustained as a *renewable asset class*.

## Mapping Competence to Pipeline Stages

Leadership readiness is not a mystery; it is measurable growth across domains. This process is a direct response to the confidence-competence gap (Chapter 1) because it forces the organization to define and measure the distinct skills needed at each stage. Competence evolves from technical expert to enterprise leader.

Technical expertise involves a linear focus on solving defined problems (e.g., coding, accounting); leadership at the Strategic and Enterprise levels demands non-linear competence—managing ambiguity, synthesizing disparate information, and aligning political objectives with ethical duty. This systemic view is where the newly promoted Technical Expert (Chapter 5) most often fails, as their previous success formula (precision and control) actively hinders the required complexity tolerance.

The structural framework of the pipeline—the four organizational chambers described previously—only succeeds if it is fueled by a defined progression of behavioral readiness. As leaders move upward, their primary functional focus shifts, demanding mastery of increasingly complex domains. This next stage requires deliberately mapping *which* competencies are expected at *which* level of authority. The table below illustrates this conceptual roadmap, showing how an individual's focus must evolve from mere technical output toward broad organizational stewardship.

*Table 6.2 — Competency Progression Matrix*

| Stage | Core Focus | Sample Competencies | Readiness Indicators |
|---|---|---|---|
| Technical | Accuracy and execution | Subject-matter expertise, reliability, procedural compliance | Consistently meets performance metrics; mentors peers on process. |
| Supervisory | People management and communication | Delegation, coaching, feedback, conflict resolution | Conducts regular 1:1s; closes 80 % of performance plans on time. |
| Strategic | Systems thinking and alignment | Budget stewardship, cross-unit collaboration, data-driven decisions | Connects budgets to outcomes; leads multi-department initiatives. |
| Enterprise | Vision and culture | Policy influence, ethics, equity, public trust | Shapes organizational values; mentors next-generation leaders. |

The challenge of ensuring competence is not merely documenting it in a matrix; it lies in institutionalizing the process by which leaders acquire and integrate these behavioral skills. This process relies on a dynamic developmental model known as the Readiness Framework. This framework posits that true readiness advances through iterative **learning loops: exposure → application → feedback → reflection**. Each promotion resets the loop at a higher altitude. By institutionalizing these learning loops—rather than leaving them to personal luck—pipelines ensure that the complexity of the ECQs (Chapter 5) is broken down into manageable, measurable developmental steps.

This transition from a rigid checklist to a fluid, sustained learning loop is the necessary foundation for the culture-building practices that follow.

## Cultivating the Readiness Culture

Pipelines thrive only in a culture that normalizes development. Formal programs matter, but informal habits make them durable. Creating this sustaining culture requires intentional practices that embed learning, feedback, and psychological safety directly into daily work. This means treating every manager as a developer of talent and institutionalizing the relational support mechanisms that supplement formal training. The core components of a readiness culture—specifically **Mentorship as Behavioral Transfer**, **Coaching and Deliberate Practice**, and ensuring **Psychological Safety and Learning**—are the essential mechanisms that transform theoretical competencies into embedded organizational habits, ensuring the entire workforce remains a managed asset class.

### Mentorship as Behavioral Transfer

Research by Allen and Eby (2010) confirms that structured mentoring accelerates leadership self-efficacy and retention. The most effective systems pair mentors and mentees across functions, breaking silos and fostering shared understanding. This directly addresses the Peer-to-Boss Transition problem (Chapter 3) by giving new leaders a confidential source of advice outside their direct reporting structure. Mentoring acts as a critical behavioral transfer mechanism, moving theoretical knowledge from the classroom to practical application. It is the structured antidote to the Lack of Training (Chapter 4), providing the experiential learning loop that generic workshops omit.

### Coaching and Deliberate Practice

Coaching embeds reflection into daily work. When new supervisors debrief one critical decision per week with a senior peer, learning compounds faster than quarterly workshops ever achieve. This process is what Raelin (2016) terms reflection-in-action, moving learning from abstract memory to embedded habit.

Effective coaching compels the emerging leader to confront the identity dissonance identified in Chapter 5—the shift from technical doer to strategic enabler. It provides the psychological safety (Edmondson, 2018) necessary for the new leader to experiment with delegation, tolerate imperfection, and grow confidence without succumbing to the anxiety that leads to micromanagement.

## Psychological Safety and Learning

Edmondson (2018) identifies psychological safety as the foundation of adaptive performance. In organizations that celebrate learning from mistakes, pipelines widen; in those that punish missteps, they clog. Creating a feedback-safe environment means rewarding candor, curiosity, and incremental improvement. This cultural commitment protects the emerging leader, allowing them to fail forward without incurring the full institutional cost of a structural error.

> **Quick Check — Culture Readiness**
> - Is feedback normalized at every level?
> - Are mentors recognized in performance reviews?
> - Do new leaders receive onboarding plans that include coaching and reflection checkpoints?

# Measuring and Sustaining the System

What gets measured shapes what gets maintained. Pipelines falter when development outcomes are invisible, risking the return of the Managerial Tuition (Chapter 2). Measuring pipeline health is a fiduciary duty that extends beyond mere reporting; it represents the organizational commitment to protecting and renewing its most valuable asset: leadership capacity. If the results of development remain abstract, investment will become vulnerable to budget cuts, and systemic competence will erode. Sustaining the pipeline requires continuous, objective measurement that looks beyond glossy training catalogs to assess the actual health and resilience of the leadership ecosystem. This mandates a shift from evaluating simple *activity* (e.g., number of workshops held) to assessing concrete *results* (e.g., capability continuity and risk mitigation).

## Core Metrics for Capability Continuity

Measuring organizational health requires looking beyond simple output metrics to assess the system's resilience across five non-negotiable domains:

- **Readiness Ratio:** This metric tracks the percentage of key supervisory, strategic, and enterprise roles that have at least one identified and actively prepared successor. It provides a direct, quantitative assessment of the organization's vulnerability to sudden departures and its effectiveness in mitigating the Systemic Drivers of Incompetence (Chapter 3).
- **Retention Rate (of Leaders):** This measures the proportion of new leaders retained after a defined period (typically two years) in their role, serving as a critical indicator of the efficacy of Transition Support and the cost of Managerial Tuition. High retention rates for participants who receive coaching and mentorship (Chapter 4) demonstrate the return on developmental investment.
- **Diversity Index (across Leadership Levels):** This measures the demographic spread across all leadership levels against organizational representation goals. It serves as an objective metric for achieving Social Equity (Chapter 2) and proves that the pipeline successfully dismantles the informal, selective sponsorship patterns that plague merit systems.
- **Engagement Score (Developmental Opportunity):** This tracks employee perception of access to developmental opportunities, structured coaching, and fair promotion pathways. It is a critical leading indicator of organizational culture health and the workforce's belief in the Merit Principle, reflecting the effectiveness of Cultivating the Readiness Culture.
- **Ethical Climate Index:** This tracks the frequency of reported vs. resolved ethical concerns related to management (e.g., fairness, abuse of authority, favoritism). Its measure provides quantitative insight into the Ethical Duty of Care (Chapter 9) and the integrity of the selection and performance management systems across the organization.

The functional and ethical vitality of the leadership pipeline is revealed by these quantitative measures. Yet, these metrics capture the *health of the system*, not necessarily the *impact of the training programs* themselves. To justify the investment in multimodal development (Chapter 4) and sustain the culture of readiness, organizations must directly connect learning activities to measurable improvements in leader behavior and organizational outcomes. This requires moving beyond subjective satisfaction scores and employing a rigorous evaluation framework.

## Evaluating Impact

To ensure that resources dedicated to the pipeline are yielding true capability, evaluation must be strategic. Public organizations must adopt frameworks that measure functional transfer, moving beyond simple engagement scores to assess behavior and results. The most widely adopted model for this purpose, developed by Kirkpatrick and Kirkpatrick (2016), identifies four distinct levels of evaluation. While many organizations stop at Level 1 (Reaction) and Level 2 (Learning), effective pipeline management demands objective measurement at the two highest levels: Public organizations must strive for Level 3 (Behavior) and Level 4 (Results) to justify the investment.

- **Level 3 (Behavior):** This level measures the extent to which participants actually apply the new knowledge and skills learned in the pipeline back on the job. This requires observing and documenting specific, desired leadership actions, such as conducting a structured delegation huddle, delivering candid performance feedback, or successfully closing a conflict. This level directly counters the Lack of Training (Chapter 4) by verifying that awareness has translated into sustained changes in daily practice.
- **Level 4 (Results):** This level measures the ultimate, tangible benefit to the organization or community resulting from the leader's change in behavior. Examples include measurable improvements in service delivery and morale, such as a reduction in avoidable audit findings, faster case processing times, improved retention rates for subordinate staff, or measurable gains in public trust. This is the highest form of

accountability, justifying the investment by proving the pipeline's contribution to mission success.

> **Practice Note — Measuring What Matters**
>
> Evaluate outcomes, not optics. Healthy pipelines show fewer emergency hires, higher engagement, and greater internal diversity—not just glossy training catalogs. This measurement shift is the core action required to prevent the return of the Managerial Tuition (Chapter 2).

## Ethical Governance: The Social Equity Link

Ethical stewardship requires that opportunity be transparent and equitable. Pipelines are not just compliance tools; they are instruments of social equity. This systemic reality ensures that social equity becomes an objective performance metric, not a subjective value statement. By mandating transparency (visible criteria) and intentional resource allocation (coaching for high-potential, underrepresented talent), the pipeline actively combats the selective attrition pattern and reliance on informal sponsorship that plagues most organizations.

- **Transparency:** Entry criteria and evaluation rubrics must be visible and consistently applied. This means moving beyond vague qualifications to publish clear behavioral indicators for every stage of advancement. Transparent processes dismantle the perception of favoritism (Chapter 3) and build foundational trust that the system operates on meritocratic principles, not personal connections.
- **Equity:** Equitable pipelines allocate resources—time, coaching, visibility—to under-represented talent, not just to those already visible. This is a conscious, active intervention to counteract the implicit bias that often channels developmental opportunities toward established networks, ensuring that high-potential employees from all backgrounds receive the formal support needed to acquire tacit management knowledge (Chapter 4).
- **Accountability:** Leader evaluations must be tied to how well they cultivate others, not just deliver technical results. This shifts the focus from individual heroism to collective capacity building, making the

development of subordinate staff a measurable, professional mandate. This metric actively combats the micromanagement tendency by rewarding delegation and coaching behavior.
- **Stewardship:** Developmental investments must be linked directly to the ASPA Code of Ethics (2013) principles: advancing the public interest, upholding law, promoting participation, strengthening social equity, and advancing professional excellence. This links the organization's investment in its pipeline directly to its broader ethical mandate, reframing competence development

These four ethical mandates—Transparency, Equity, Accountability, and Stewardship—collectively ensure that the selection process reflects the organization's highest public values. They transform the pipeline from a simple HR tool into an institutional mechanism for strengthening social equity and reinforcing public trust. When these principles are formalized into practice, the systemic cycle of incompetence is finally broken, yielding measurable returns on ethical governance.

**Case Study — Alameda Plains County Leadership Academy**

When Alameda Plains County recognized that its management bench was thinning, it saw two risks: losing institutional knowledge by hiring externally, and manufacturing incompetence by defaulting to seniority internally (Chapter 3). To mitigate the latter risk, the County launched a leadership academy spanning three sectors—county government, community health, and local nonprofits.

The program was not designed to promote people solely based on completion; it was designed to test and train readiness before promotion. Participants spent one year rotating through modules on supervision, budgeting, ethics, and equity. Each cohort completed a cross-agency capstone addressing a shared service challenge such as homelessness response or workforce housing. This experiential component functioned as a structured stretch assignment, forcing participants to exercise Strategic and Enterprise-level competencies (Chapter 5) before receiving the title.

Outcomes after two years: of graduates were promoted internally, demonstrating preparedness; retention of emerging leaders was up compared with nonparticipants; and three cross-agency projects were institutionalized as standing programs.

***Lesson tags:*** Structured preparation neutralizes the danger of promoting from within. Promotion was earned through measurable capability, not seniority. Intentional investment creates measurable capacity and strengthens ethical governance.

## Conclusion – Designing for Continuity

Leadership pipelines institutionalize what ad-hoc promotion systems ignore: that leadership is not inherited; it is engineered. Continuity is not luck—it is logistics. By turning readiness into routine measurement, feedback, and equity, organizations ensure that competence endures beyond individuals. The ultimate value of the pipeline is this: it is the systemic antidote to the confidence-competence gap.

Chapter 7 continues this design from the organizational to the personal level, focusing on the tools and practices emerging leaders can use to own their development within the pipeline they now inhabit.

# Chapter 7 - Tools for Emerging Leaders

*Growth is deliberate; competence evolves through design*

This chapter shifts the focus from the organization's responsibility for creating pipelines (Chapter 6) to the individual leader's responsibility for self-development. It is a practical field guide for early- to mid-level leaders learning to convert organizational opportunity into sustained personal capability. This chapter turns from the organizational system to the individual responsibility for self-development.

## Owning the Learning Curve

Every new leader steps into uncertainty. The moment promotion becomes reality, the familiar comfort of technical mastery gives way to the complexity of leading others. Success now depends less on what one can do personally and more on what one can enable others to do. This shift demands profound humility: the willingness to become a beginner again while everyone assumes expertise. The speed at which one adapts, reflects, and learns determines the degree of confidence others will have in that leadership.

This is not a passive process; research by Day and Dragoni (2015) confirms that effective leadership growth occurs through deliberate practice—regular feedback, structured reflection, and incremental experimentation, not merely passive experience. The first responsibility of an emerging leader is, therefore, to actively own the learning curve.

This adaptation requires key psychological multipliers. The first is **Learning Agility**, which is the core competency of adaptive leadership—the ability to learn quickly from new experiences and apply that learning to novel situations. The second is a **Growth Mindset** (Dweck, 2006). This mindset is the psychological fuel that overcomes the identity dissonance (Chapter 5) inherent in the shift from "doer" to "enabler," reinforcing the belief that one's abilities are developed through effort. This conviction that competence is cultivable directly counters the fear of failure that often leads to micromanagement. Leaders who view setbacks as "data for the next rep" accelerate readiness faster than those who treat them as verdicts, bolstering their sense of self-efficacy (Bandura, 1997), which is the belief in one's own capability to execute the actions necessary to manage prospective situations. The leader must deliberately trade the comfort of defending technical mastery for the productive discomfort of seeking growth.

The necessity of the learning loop—combining assessment, challenge, and support—demands that the emerging leader first achieve radical self-awareness. Before any organization can intervene with training or mentorship, the individual must pause to audit their own behaviors and identify where the old success formula is still hindering them. The following quick check forces this immediate confrontation with the distinction between doing and leading.

> **Quick Check – Am I Learning or Performing?**
>
> The key to managing this adaptation is accurate self-diagnosis. Use these questions to determine whether your current focus is building future capacity or simply defending past competence:
>
> - When was the last time you actively sought a task you knew you might fail at?
> - Do you measure success by how well you accomplish your tasks, or by the challenging new skills you acquire?
> - Are you investing in development (growth) or defending your mastery (performance)?

Moving from this essential moment of self-reflection, the organization and the individual need a common language to define the required skills. Competence in leadership is not merely a philosophical attitude; it is a measurable, behavioral set of capabilities that must be explicitly taught and assessed.

## Essential Leadership Practices

The conceptual shift from *doing* to *leading* (Chapter 5) must be translated into portable practices—the disciplined habits that form the non-negotiable core of effective, ethical leadership. These five daily habits address the skill deficits that typically cause managerial failure in the early stages post-promotion. Leadership excellence is, ultimately, less about innate traits than about disciplined habits.

- **Clarify Purpose:** The expert focuses on **correctness**; the leader focuses on **meaning**. Effective leaders continually translate the organizational mission into meaningful daily work by articulating not only *what* must be done but *why it matters*. Denhardt et al. (2013) call this the essence of public service motivation, anchoring every decision in values that serve the collective good. This consistent practice counters the slow decision-making and initiative fatigue (Chapter 2) that plague teams lacking clear direction.
- **Communicate with Intention:** Words shape trust, and communication is the currency of competence. This practice requires active listening, framing difficult conversations constructively, and establishing candid feedback loops that function not just downward (giving instruction), but upward (managing the supervisor's expectations) and laterally (aligning with peers). Clear expectations, transparent reasoning, and consistent follow-through build credibility faster than eloquence.
- **Coach and Develop Others:** The central transition from *doing* to *designing* is manifest in delegation, which must be performed as **coaching**. Leaders must move beyond simply assigning tasks toward capacity building, ensuring that every assignment is a developmental opportunity for the staff member. This corrects the toxic micromanagement failure pattern by intentionally transferring knowledge and authority, making staff competent enough to run their own tasks. Raelin (2016) argues that leaders grow competence in others through work-based learning—reflection in action, not after it.
- **Decide and Own:** Technical analysis provides inputs; leadership provides judgment. Decisions reveal ethics. This practice involves

balancing quantitative analysis with qualitative factors (ethics, stakeholder impact, political risk). Leaders who acknowledge uncertainty yet act with integrity earn more durable trust than those who disguise doubt with bravado. Emotional intelligence (Goleman, 1998) is the emotional foundation for judgment, combining self-awareness and self-regulation. Crucially, the leader must own the resulting decision—a fundamental shift from recommending solutions to managing the consequences.

- **Reflect and Reset:** Leadership maturity requires constant self-calibration and discipline. Leaders must commit to continuous improvement through brief, daily reflection cycles—a habit that transforms mistakes from crises into learning opportunities, bolstering psychological safety (Edmondson, 2018). Sustainable leaders learn, adjust, and move on.

These five practices—from clarifying purpose to disciplined reflection—define the minimum viable competence for the new leader. Yet, even the most intentional habits cannot be sustained in isolation. The pursuit of growth is inherently relational, depending on accurate data to inform reflection and diverse partnerships to accelerate learning. Therefore, the deliberate practice of leadership must be immediately paired with the proactive design of a personalized developmental network. This network transforms isolated effort into supported, systematic growth, ensuring the individual leader has the external systems necessary to sustain internal competence.

## Building Feedback and Support Systems

Because the organizational pipeline (Chapter 6) often has gaps—particularly around personalized coaching and high-stakes mentorship—the individual leader must take proactive ownership of their own development. This means consciously constructing the essential support infrastructure necessary for continuous growth. Rather than waiting for the organization to provide a perfect system, the leader deliberately builds a feedback ecosystem tailored to their unique needs and designed to counter the isolation and blind spots inherent in any new role. This approach converts passive hope into active strategy.

## Differentiating Roles in the Developmental Network

Effective leaders understand that reliance on a single supervisor for all support creates a distorted mirror. They cultivate a diverse support network to provide different types of capital and actively counter the isolation of the new role. Cultivating these four primary roles deliberately is essential for accelerating competence and ensuring accountability:

- **Mentors:** Mentors offer long-term, career-spanning advice, wisdom, and retrospective perspective. Their importance lies in transferring tacit knowledge—the unspoken rules of success, cultural nuances, and political context that are never written down. The absence of a mentor leaves an emerging leader susceptible to repeating historical mistakes and misinterpreting organizational signals, slowing career navigation.
- **Coaches:** Coaches provide intensive, short-term support focused on immediate behavioral change and skill transfer (Raelin, 2016). They are instrumental in embedding reflection-in-action, observing the leader's performance in real time (e.g., managing a conflict) and providing fast, targeted feedback. The lack of a coach means the leader's mistakes harden into habits, allowing the micromanagement failure pattern to persist unchallenged.
- **Sponsors:** Sponsors use their positional influence to create opportunities for advancement and visibility. They are the necessary counterweight to the Cultural Taboo (Chapter 1) that stifles candid discussion about promotion. By advocating for their protégé in high-level discussions and securing stretch assignments (Chapter 6), sponsors dismantle barriers to advancement. Without a sponsor, high potential often remains invisible and untapped.
- **Peers:** Peers offer crucial reality checks, emotional support, and perspective on organizational culture. They provide a safe space to share vulnerabilities and process the emotional toll of leadership (moral injury, burnout). The power of this network is that it counters the isolation of the new role by normalizing mutual learning and accountability. The successful leader must proactively seek the critique: *What am I not seeing?*

Cultivating this network immediately clarifies the need for emotional intelligence (EQ) and ethical competence. The feedback received—whether it concerns poor delegation from a coach or a difficult political decision from a peer—is useless unless the leader possesses the self-awareness and courage to absorb it, process the dissonance, and change behavior.

This capacity for ethical and emotional self-management is not merely a desirable trait; it is a core readiness skill that prevents systemic failure. The next section explores how these internal capacities function as the non-negotiable tools of responsible leadership, acting as the protective layer against the ethical and human costs detailed in Chapter 2. The psychological courage gained through self-management is immediately tested by a system of unspoken rules.

## Ethical and Emotional Competence

Ethical judgment and emotional management are not optional additions; they are the core readiness skills that prevent ethical failures (Chapter 9) and mitigate people costs (Chapter 2). For the emerging leader, the ability to regulate one's internal state and apply ethical principles is the protective armor that sustains leadership influence. These internal capacities are the non-negotiable tools of responsible leadership, distinguishing the thoughtful enabler from the impulsive manager.

### Emotional Competence

Emotional Intelligence (EQ), as defined by Daniel Goleman (1998), is the capacity to manage one's own emotions and those of others. These capacities transform raw authority into lasting influence. Without them, the high performer is likely to fracture team trust. Leaders must deliberately develop:

- **Self-Awareness:** This is the foundational skill of EQ—the capacity to accurately perceive and understand one's own emotional state, triggers, strengths, and weaknesses. It is the crucial antidote to the confidence-competence gap (Chapter 1) because it allows the leader to recognize areas of unreadiness, manage personal anxiety, and seek coaching before failure occurs. Without self-awareness, misaligned

competence persists as the leader rationalizes mistakes rather than addressing them.
- **Self-Regulation:** This involves managing stress, impulses, and negative emotional reactions, especially when facing high-stakes conflict or policy setbacks. It is the internal resilience required when dealing with the ambiguity of adaptive challenges and resistance (Heifetz and Linsky, 2017). A leader lacking self-regulation will project their own stress onto the team, leading directly to the toxic micromanagement and burnout patterns cataloged in Chapter 2.
- **Empathy:** The ability to understand the perspective, motivations, and emotional state of staff and stakeholders. Empathy is crucial for managing teams through organizational change, addressing conflict fairly, and recognizing the early signs of staff disengagement. This capacity ensures leaders address the human costs of policy decisions proactively.

The mastery of these three emotional competencies—self-awareness, self-regulation, and empathy—provides the internal scaffolding necessary for ethical conduct. Without this foundational capacity to manage self and relate to others, the leader cannot fulfill the higher moral obligations of the role. This commitment to managing influence and minimizing harm transforms personal competence into public integrity, directly addressing the ethical risks inherent in public leadership.

## Ethical Stewardship and the Duty of Care

The ethical challenge in public service is acute. Drawing on Denhardt et al. (2013), leaders must practice stewardship—managing their influence and resources responsibly in service of the public good. This commitment includes:

- **Emotional Stewardship:** This concept (informed by research on burnout and moral injury) demands that leaders manage their own behavior and influence to avoid creating burnout or moral injury in the workforce (Maslach & Leiter, 2022). A leader practicing emotional stewardship ensures their stress does not become the staff's burden, protecting the health of the team as a core asset.

- **Procedural Justice:** This involves ensuring fairness, transparency, and consistency in daily decision-making (e.g., performance reviews, resource allocation). Procedural justice fulfills the deontological duty to process (Chapter 9) by making decisions defensible and predictable. Its absence fuels cynicism, leading staff to believe outcomes are based on favoritism rather than merit (Chapter 3).

The development of this internal ethical and emotional scaffolding prepares the leader for the final, and often most treacherous, external domain: organizational culture. The psychological courage gained through self-management is immediately tested by a system of unspoken rules. Leadership does not happen in a vacuum; it occurs within a culture that may actively reward the very traits (like silence, compliance, or political loyalty) that undermine ethical leadership. Therefore, the capable leader must now apply their developed self-awareness and ethical competence to systematically diagnose and strategically engage the environment around them. The next section explores how the capable leader must apply their developed self-awareness to diagnose and strategically engage the environment around them.

## Navigating Organizational Culture

The development of internal readiness—mastery over one's emotions and commitment to ethical principles—prepares the leader for the final, and often most treacherous, external domain: organizational culture. Leadership does not happen in a vacuum; it occurs within a dynamic system of spoken rules, unspoken norms, and deeply embedded historical practices. The emerging leader must become culturally literate to maximize effectiveness, avoid becoming a "leadership drainer" (Chapter 5), and ensure their actions align with the organization's true operating code.

### Culture Diagnostics and Mapping

Organizational culture is a complex landscape that must be systematically diagnosed. It is composed of three observable layers: artifacts (visible symbols and norms), espoused values (stated mission and official rules), and underlying assumptions (the unspoken rules that truly drive behavior). Mastering this layer requires cultural literacy and Diagnosis—the deliberate effort to identify the unspoken rules of The Cost of Silence (Chapter 1). Culture Mapping is the applied tool for identifying these visible norms, unspoken rules, and strategic leverage points for influence. By diagnosing culture accurately, new leaders ensure their initiatives won't be sabotaged by misalignment with deeply held institutional beliefs.

## Leadership Tool - Culture Mapping Worksheet

The following tool, which is detailed for fieldwork in Appendix C, serves as a crucial framework for systematic cultural diagnosis:

*Table 7.1 - Cultural Mapping Worksheet*

| Element | Examples / Questions | Implications for Action |
|---|---|---|
| Artifacts | Dress code, office layout, meeting rituals | What do these symbols say about hierarchy or openness? |
| Espoused Values | Stated mission, diversity statements, strategic plans | Where do words and actions diverge? |
| Underlying Assumptions | Who is trusted? Who decides? What is rewarded? | How can I navigate respectfully while modeling transparency? |

## Balancing Dissent with Conformity

Adaptive leadership often requires principled dissent—challenging existing assumptions or organizational flaws that undermine the public mission. This is where the leader's internal resilience is tested. Leaders must learn to balance **conformity** (respecting institutional memory and hierarchy) with principled dissent (driving necessary change). Successfully navigating this tension—avoiding simple rebellion on one hand, and blind compliance on the other—is the essence of cultural intelligence. This principled adaptability—respecting existing norms while modeling and introducing healthier ones—is the mechanism by which positive change is sustained within a resilient, often resistant, public environment.

## Sustaining Growth and Resilience

Leadership maturity is not a destination; it is the habit of deliberate practice. The final set of tools focuses on endurance—strategies leaders must adopt for long-term well-being and continuous improvement to ensure their personal growth keeps pace with the demands of the pipeline. After building the necessary external networks and mastering emotional competence, the final challenge for the emerging leader is achieving psychological sustainability. The complexity, ambiguity, and chronic political nature of public service create an environment where burnout and moral injury are ever-present risks, threatening to erode competence faster than technical ignorance. Therefore, the capable leader must treat personal resilience not as a luxury, but as a strategic asset that protects both the individual's effectiveness and the organizational capacity. This demands intentional practice in managing energy, maintaining purpose alignment, and formalizing continuous improvement cycles.

### Resilience and Burnout Prevention

Burnout (Maslach & Leiter, 2022) erodes competence faster than ignorance. Leaders who fail to manage their personal energy risk becoming a toxic leadership drainer (Chapter 5), creating the very burnout challenge in their teams that they themselves are experiencing. Preventing this requires integrating resilience research into daily practice. This involves two key efforts:

1. **Purpose Alignment:** The daily, complex work of public service is fueled by mission. Leaders must consistently link their daily tasks, even the tedious ones, back to the fundamental public purpose. This alignment provides the necessary energy to resist fatigue and sustain resilience when facing setbacks.
2. **Reflective Practice:** Committing to the reflective cycles (daily/weekly/quarterly) is a mechanism for mental hygiene. It prevents small errors and grievances from compounding into fatigue and promotes the mental clarity necessary for strategic decision-making.

**Practice Note – Micro-Habits for Endurance**

- Schedule structured reflection (10 minutes daily) to process emotional costs and prevent moral injury.
- Implement a "Stop-Doing" list (weekly) to intentionally delegate tasks and avoid reverting to individual technical performance.
- Cultivate mindfulness or exercise to sustain the Self-Regulation essential for effective crisis leadership.

## Personal Development Planning (PDP)

Formalizing one's commitment to growth transforms passive hope into an actionable, measurable strategy. The Personal Development Plan (PDP) is the critical document that links the individual's aspirations to the pipeline's demands (Chapter 6). It is not a suggestion; it is the personalized blueprint for building **prospective capability** (Chapter 1). A robust PDP must be specific, actionable, and aligned with the organizational reality. Leaders must encourage and commit to creating a plan that links individual goals directly to the measurable competencies of the next stage in their career. This formalized structure links individual growth to the system's needs, ensuring that personal development serves the goal of organizational capability.

The PDP ensures that the investment of time and energy is deliberate, not random. It requires the leader to articulate not just *what* skill they lack, but *how* they will acquire it, *who* will coach them, and *what metric* (Level 4, Kirkpatrick) will prove the skill has been transferred into reliable behavior. By formalizing this document, the individual leader takes complete ownership of their advancement, shifting the focus from simply *being available* for promotion to *being measurably ready* for it.

## Conclusion – From Participant to Practitioner

Leadership maturity is not a destination; it is the habit of deliberate practice. The tools and frameworks discussed in this chapter empower the emerging leader to move beyond being a passive participant in a pipeline and become an active practitioner of their own growth. The journey from individual contributor to effective leader is marked by daily intentionality—

clarifying purpose, seeking honest feedback, exercising empathy, and refining judgment. Leadership is learned behavior performed on behalf of others. The individual effort of self-development is the necessary counterpart to the organizational commitment detailed in Chapter 6.

This pivotal chapter marks the transition where personal mastery scales into shared practice. The habits you've built—clarifying purpose, designing feedback, navigating culture, protecting energy—multiply when peers adopt them together. This collective adoption transforms development from a personal project into an organizational culture, readying the system for resilience.

The next chapter, Chapter 8, will close the diagnostic loop by focusing on this shared responsibility and delivering the final Call to Action.

# Chapter 8 – From Individual Excellence to Collective Leadership

*Leadership maturity is built on one intentional act at a time.*

This chapter completes the developmental arc of the book, transitioning from personal readiness (Chapter 7) to systemic capability. It shows how the habits of trust, reflection, and ethical accountability must be institutionalized across the organization, converting individual competence into a resilient, shared culture.

## The Shift from Me to We

Every leader's development begins as a personal pursuit (Chapter 7). But organizational resilience depends on converting that individual learning into **collective competence**—shared habits of trust, reflection, and coordinated action. When teams move from personal heroics to collaborative mastery, leadership stops being a position and becomes a practice.

This transition is fundamentally counter-cultural in hierarchical organizations, where positional identity and risk aversion often hinder collaboration. The conceptual shift moves from the simplicity of individual ownership to the complexity of interdependence. Raelin (2016) calls this **leaderful practice**: multiple people engaging in leadership together, with mutual openness, compassion, and shared accountability. Likewise, Day, Gronn, and Salas (2004) describe **leadership capacity** as a team property rather than an individual trait. The question shifts from *Who leads?* to *How do we lead together?* This conversion of personal reflection into organizational output creates **networks of readiness**, the final structural defense against manufactured incompetence.

A practical example comes from a mid-sized city's emergency-response project. To combat burnout and positional rigidity, the project management office mandated rotating leadership. Each week, a different section chief facilitated the cross-functional meeting, applying the same agenda template. Rotating responsibility revealed latent strengths, normalized feedback, and built appreciation for the system rather than the seat.

## Building Trust and Psychological Safety

Trust is the social infrastructure of collective leadership. Teams that trust can challenge ideas, admit errors, and engage in constructive conflict without threatening personal identity or damaging relationships. Without this foundation of safety, the open dialogue necessary for learning and innovation immediately collapses, and staff revert to the Culture of Silence (Chapter 1)—the pervasive organizational habit of withholding critical information out of fear. This silence is the primary mechanism that enables manufactured incompetence to persist.

### Psychological Safety as a Collective Asset

The necessary antidote to the Culture of Silence is psychological safety. According to Edmondson (2018), psychological safety—the belief that candor will not be punished—is the single strongest predictor of learning behavior in groups. It transforms mistakes from grounds for discipline into data points for improvement. In a compliance-driven sector like public service, generating this safety is the leader's primary relational duty. Building this trust requires two-way accountability:

### The Leader's Proactive Duty (Modeling the Path

The leader must actively and consistently model vulnerability and commitment to learning, recognizing that safety is granted by authority, not earned by subordinates. This involves:

- **Admitting Error:** Openly acknowledging one's own oversights or mistakes signals to the entire team that the focus is on the system, not the individual. This act of ethical vulnerability directly counters the confidence-competence gap (Chapter 1) by normalizing imperfection and demonstrating that learning is valued over flawless performance.

- **Seeking Critique:** Proactively asking the team, "What system failure allowed this to happen?" or "What am I missing?" (rather than waiting for issues to surface). This habit ensures that the leader's blind spots are intentionally surfaced and addressed, preventing the persistence of organizational risk that stems from the leader's authority.
- **Equitable Engagement:** Distributing airtime equitably and ensuring every voice—especially dissenting or junior voices—is heard before decisions harden. This practice reinforces the principle of procedural justice and prevents the systemic failures that occur when critical information is filtered out by hierarchy or risk aversion.
- **Follow-Through:** Consistently acting on team input, thereby validating the risk the team took in offering candor. If a leader solicits input but fails to integrate it or explain why it was declined, the Culture of Silence (Chapter 1) will immediately return.

## The Team's Reciprocal Role (Sustaining the Norm)

The team must reciprocate by converting the psychological safety granted by the leader into collective responsibility. This behavioral shift ensures that vulnerability is used for mission advancement, not personal gain or attack. This includes:

- **Using Candor for the Mission:** Utilizing the safety to engage in principled dissent against flawed ideas, rather than using the openness for personal attacks or gossip. This demonstrates a commitment to the public mission and actively supports the leader in upholding the duty of care to the process.
- **Focusing on Process:** Shifting the automatic cognitive reaction from "Who's to blame?" to "What process failed?". This crucial reframing mechanism redirects energy away from punitive individual defense toward systemic, organizational learning.
- **Active Learning:** Engaging in after-action reviews (AARs) and sharing insights openly, thereby making the learning visible to the entire group. This commitment turns individual experience into collective competence, strengthening the team's ability to handle

future challenges and reinforcing the norms of continuous improvement.

Trust grows when leaders model vulnerability, and the entire team maintains the norm that learning outweighs ego. The outcome is measurable: High-trust teams spend less time protecting personal reputation and far more time focused on improving operational results.

> **Quick Check – Team Trust Indicators**
> - Are team members willing to admit mistakes publicly?
> - Do meetings include genuine disagreement that ends in clarity, not silence?
> - When problems surface, is the first question "What happened?" or "Who's to blame?"

## Shared Accountability and Decision-Making

Traditional hierarchies equate leadership with control. Collective systems, however, fundamentally re-frame this dynamic as stewardship—a shared accountability for outcomes. While responsibilities remain individual (each person owns their specific task), accountability becomes mutual (the team collectively shares ownership of the final result and the learning derived from it).

This requires a profound change in mindset for the emerging leader. They must actively shift from **ownership**—the tendency to guard turf, micromanage resources, and focus solely on personal output—to **stewardship**, which is managing resources and influence for the common good. This emphasis on shared accountability underscores interdependence. Success hinges not just on the individual's technical output but on the team's capacity to deliver, making collective competence a strategic imperative. This shift directly counters the control failures that lead to the micromanagement trap (Chapter 2).

### Stewardship vs. Control: The Mindset Shift

The failure to embrace stewardship often sabotages collective work. A leader operating from a mindset of *control* views collaboration as a risk to be managed and seeks to eliminate variation. A leader operating from a mindset of *stewardship*, by contrast, views collaboration as an opportunity for learning and actively seeks out diverse perspectives. The steward understands that while authority is delegated to them, the mission belongs to the public, and the success belongs to the team. This distinction is vital for public service, where the core ethical duty (Chapter 9) is to manage resources on behalf of citizens, not personal ambition.

## Governance through Team Charters

Well-designed, mature teams make shared accountability explicit through governance mechanisms—formal agreements that clarify interdependence. These are often established through Team Charters that define purpose, norms, decision rules, and escalation paths. These governance mechanisms replace the ambiguity of informal politics (which favors favoritism and silence, Chapter 3) with transparency, ensuring that accountability is based on a mutually agreed-upon process. Team charters prevent collaboration from devolving into a diffusion of responsibility, ensuring that when collective action is required, the methodology for decision-making is already established.

> **Practice Note – Team Charter Essentials**
>
> To ensure the team charter functions as a living governance tool—tight enough for accountability, loose enough for adaptation—it must address the core friction points in collective work:
>
> - **Purpose:** What mission binds us beyond functional goals? (Ensures alignment with public service motivation).
> - **Norms:** How will we communicate, resolve conflict, and document decisions? (Creates psychological safety).
> - **Decision Rules:** Which decisions require consensus, consultation, or delegation? (Prevents slow decision-making).
> - **Escalation Paths:** When impasse occurs, what is the process for resolution? (Prevents initiative fatigue).

## Learning Teams and Continuous Improvement

Collective leadership thrives where teams learn as naturally as they execute. Senge (2006) called such organizations "learning organizations": places where people continually expand their capacity to create desired results. This requires embedding structured reflection into the workflow, actively ensuring that mistakes are treated as data points for system improvement, not grounds for blame. This practice is the counter-cultural norm that finally overcomes the Culture of Silence (Chapter 1).

## After-Action Reviews (AARs): Diagnosing Process Failure

The **After-Action Review (AAR)** is the foundational tool for transforming experience into collective intelligence. Originally a military discipline, the AAR is a brief, disciplined, and mandatory process conducted immediately after an event—whether successful or failed—to diagnose *process* rather than assign *blame*. A key principle is that the focus must be on what happened and why, bypassing personal defense mechanisms. In a public service context, AARs are essential for turning a service failure, a difficult public meeting, or a failed grant application into a system-wide learning event. This shifts the team's cognitive default from "Who's to blame?" to "What system design allowed this error?", ensuring that the learning is systemic and repeatable.

## Peer Learning Cycles: Cultivating Reflection-in-Action

Complementing the backward-looking AAR is the forward-looking **Peer Learning Cycle**. This mechanism provides structured time for reflection-in-action (Raelin, 2016) —pausing briefly *within* work to ask what is being learned while doing it. Peer learning embeds improvement culture through structured time with colleagues, offering diverse viewpoints that expose blind spots. This practice contrasts reflection-in-action with double-loop learning (Senge, 2006), which demands questioning underlying assumptions rather than merely fixing visible errors. By institutionalizing regular time for peer feedback, teams actively foster psychological safety and ensure that the individual growth habits from Chapter 7 multiply across the collective.

## Leadership Tool - Team Learning Canvas

To facilitate this structured reflection, teams require simple, powerful tools. The **Team Learning Canvas** ensures that the outcome of these reviews—whether an AAR or a peer learning cycle—is captured in a format that mandates clear action and accountability. Teams that use this canvas monthly turn reflection into infrastructure. They learn in real time instead of in hindsight.

*Table 8.1 — Leadership Tool - Team Learning Canvas*

| Stage | Key Questions | Intended Outcome |
|---|---|---|
| 1. Event/Action | What did we do? Who was involved? | Shared factual account |
| 2. Insights | What patterns or surprises emerged? | Collective understanding |
| 3. Experiments | What one thing will we try differently? | Small, safe innovation |
| 4. Next Steps | Who owns what by when? | Clear accountability |

## Ethical Culture and Inclusion

Ethical culture is the glue that holds shared leadership together. When fairness, respect, and voice are protected, collaboration endures even under pressure. This operationalizes the principle of stewardship: exercising authority in service of others. Inclusion ensures every relevant voice is heard before decisions harden. The ASPA Code of Ethics (2013) reinforces the same duty—advance the public interest, strengthen social equity, and promote ethical organizations. In collective leadership, these are daily tests: *Is the process by which we lead as just as the outcomes we pursue?* Diverse teams generate better problem framing—but only if the culture is safe enough for those perspectives to surface.

## Moral Courage and Ethical Vigilance

Ethical vigilance is a systemic competence. It is the organizational skill of actively monitoring and correcting ethical boundaries, ensuring that daily decision-making aligns with the public mandate. Teams must have the moral courage (Kidder, 1995)—the willingness to stand up for core ethical values despite the risk of personal cost—to challenge ethical slippage or systemic failures. This concept moves the ethics discussion far beyond simple compliance, transforming the organization's moral stance from passive adherence to active defense.

This active form of ethics moves the Duty of Care (Chapter 9) from a theoretical concept to an active team norm, where challenging a poor decision is viewed not as insubordination, but as a loyal act of system protection. Moral courage serves as the critical final defense against the systemic drag of the Culture of Silence (Chapter 1), ensuring that dissenting voices are heard when accountability is most compromised. When psychological safety (discussed in this chapter) is present, moral courage can flourish, allowing the team to uphold the ethical principles mandated by the ASPA Code of Ethics (2013) even when political pressure or financial temptation suggests otherwise. This competency is essential because, in public service, a failure of ethics quickly becomes a failure of mission delivery and public trust (Chapter 2).

The concepts of Shared Accountability and Ethical Vigilance are theoretical mandates until they are tested by real-world pressure—whether financial, political, or operational. The strength of a collective leadership culture is proven not by its stated values, but by the moral courage demonstrated when core principles conflict with organizational convenience or financial gain. The following three vignettes, drawn from local government, healthcare, and the nonprofit sector, illustrate how Moral Courage and Systemic Competence translate into measurable decisions that uphold ethical stewardship and protect the mission.

### Local Government Vignette: Shared Budget Stewardship

A city finance department realized that budget preparation, traditionally owned by one technical manager, created widespread departmental resentment and misalignment. They established a Budget Stewardship Circle—a cross-functional team with rotating members from Planning, Public Works, and Finance. The group was charged with facilitating the budget process and documenting all trade-offs. The Police Chief, serving on the circle, was forced to engage with the systemic perspective (Chapter 5) rather than just their departmental silo.

The system successfully shifted ownership of the budget document from a single technician to a collectively informed group of stewards.

### Healthcare Vignette: Psychological Safety and Patient Care

In a large Veterans Affairs (VA) hospital's patient intake division, repeated errors in medication documentation were traced not to incompetence, but to fear of reporting near-misses. The Division Chief instituted Daily Huddles where the team leader began each session by openly admitting one small mistake *they* had made (e.g., misplacing a file or forgetting a form). This active modeling of vulnerability immediately generated psychological safety. Within six months, documented near-misses increased by (a leading indicator of high safety culture), while actual severe medication errors dropped by (a lagging indicator of performance).

Collective leadership proved to be the most effective compliance tool.

### Nonprofit Vignette: Defending the Mission

The board of a nationally recognized environmental nonprofit faced a tough choice when a major corporation offered a large, unrestricted donation, but with a history of documented pollution violations. The board, guided by its new charter norms, collectively decided to decline the funds, citing the need to prioritize the ASPA Code principle of advancing the public interest over organizational convenience.

This decision, though financially painful, preserved the organizational mission and reinforced public trust (Chapter 2).

## Measuring Collective Readiness

What gets measured endures. Teams committed to collective leadership track not just output but quality of collaboration and the health of their internal systems. The goal is to move beyond mere **Lagging Indicators** (e.g., turnover rate, budget variance) to **Leading Indicators** that predict organizational resilience. This holistic approach is essential for demonstrating the fiduciary return on investment for the pipeline design (Chapter 6). Core indicators must reflect the shared nature of leadership and accountability:

1. **Relational Metrics (Trust Scores):** This domain measures the safety of the social infrastructure, which is a prerequisite for collective learning. This includes survey data on psychological safety (e.g., freedom to admit mistakes) and Relational Capital (the network density of advice-seeking outside the direct chain of command). High scores indicate that the Culture of Silence (Chapter 1) has been successfully neutralized, allowing for candid communication and challenge.
2. **Structural Metrics (Flow and Capacity):** This measures how well the team manages its collective work, demonstrating operational efficiency and resource deployment. This includes tracking cross-functional project participation, efficiency of decision-making cycles, and the Readiness Ratio (the number of successors prepared for critical roles, Chapter 6). These metrics prove that the team has successfully shifted from individual control to collective process and management.
3. **Innovation Frequency:** This metric measures the team's capacity for adaptive work, assessing its ability to address "wicked problems" and environmental changes. This tracks the number of small experiments initiated and the willingness to pursue non-traditional solutions. High innovation frequency is a leading indicator that the team is comfortable with the risk inherent in learning and change.

The four-level evaluation logic proposed by Kirkpatrick and Kirkpatrick (2016) provides the necessary rigor for validating development investments.

However, for collective readiness, the focus must be on measuring the **transfer** and **impact** of shared behavior:

- **Level 1 (Reaction): How valued is our collaboration?** (Measures engagement with the process). This is the base level, assessing the participant's immediate satisfaction and perceived utility of the collective learning process (e.g., *Did they feel the AAR was valuable?*). While necessary, this metric alone cannot justify investment.
- **Level 2 (Learning): What shared skills have we gained?** (Measures knowledge acquisition, e.g., pre/post-tests on charter rules). This level verifies that participants acquired and understood the collective tools necessary for competence, such as the rules defined in the Team Charter or the principles of psychological safety.
- **Level 3 (Behavior): What norms have changed?** (Measures observable changes in team habits, e.g., *Is the Team Learning Canvas used without prompting?*). This crucial level verifies the transfer of learning by observing a sustained change in group habits, proving that the team's practice has shifted from individual ego to collective process.
- **Level 4 (Results): What organizational outcomes improved because of how we worked together?** (Measures impact on service delivery and morale). This is the final and most powerful level, linking changes in team behavior directly to organizational goals, such as cost recovery (reduced Managerial Tuition), increased service quality, or strengthened public trust.

These four levels establish the rigorous evaluation logic required for a healthy pipeline. However, translating Level 3 (Behavior) and Level 4 (Results) into routine, actionable data requires an integrated measurement tool that tracks both internal collaborative health and external mission impact. The Collective Readiness Scorecard provides the necessary mechanism to synthesize this data, ensuring the organization maintains a continuous, objective assessment of its collective leadership capacity and justifies its fiduciary investment in development.

## Leadership Tool – Collective Readiness Scorecard

To provide a substantive way of measuring readiness beyond generic evaluation, a Collective Readiness Scorecard must synthesize process health and mission outcomes. This tool directly links the team's internal behaviors (Level 3) to the public's perception (Level 4).

*Table 8.2 — Leadership Tool – Collective Readiness Scorecard*

| Indicator Domain | Metric Type (Source) | Goal & Significance |
|---|---|---|
| Trust/Safety | L3 Feedback Reciprocity Index (Peer-to-peer candor rate, using survey) | Predicts vulnerability and learning capacity (Edmondson, 2018). |
| Accountability | L3 Team Charter Compliance (Frequency of referencing norms/decision rules) | Measures adherence to shared governance and counters managerial control failures. |
| Ethical Culture | L4 Equity/Inclusion (Cross-role mentorship frequency for under-represented staff) | Validates the ethical duty of leaders to cultivate others; counters systemic inequity. |
| Mission Impact | L4 Rework Reduction Rate (Reduction in preventable errors/overtime) | Direct cost recovery metric; proves competence transfer (Chapter 2). |

## Conclusion – Leadership as Shared Practice

Collective leadership is the capstone of readiness. It transforms competence from an individual attribute into an organizational asset. When learning, trust, ethics, and measurement reinforce one another, leadership becomes the way work gets done—not the exception to it. The path from *Me* (Individual reflection, Ch. 7) to *We* (Collaborative capability, Ch. 8) completes the book's developmental arc. Sustaining that capability requires ethical vigilance; stewardship, not status, keeps the system healthy. This collective competence is **ethical competence writ large**—an organizational defense against manufactured incompetence. The final analytical task remains: tying this collective competence to the ethical vigilance necessary to protect it. Chapter 9 will now provide the final analytical framework by explicitly defining the ethical duties—the stewardship, accountability, and justice principles—that must be actively enforced to ensure these mature systems resist the old temptations of power, political influence, and systemic neglect.

# Chapter 9 – The Ethics of Leadership Misalignment

> Ethics is the final measure of every promotion.

Leadership selection and development are not value-neutral administrative tasks. They are ethical acts that determine who wields authority, how people are treated, how resources are stewarded, and whether the public can trust its institutions. When organizations promote people without preparation—or worse, on the basis of personal favor rather than bona fide readiness—they do more than create inefficiency; they commit an ethical breach. In a public service context, that breach has social equity implications and can erode confidence in government itself. Preventing "promotions into incompetence" is therefore not simply good management; it is a matter of professional ethics grounded in widely accepted public-sector norms, including the current American Society for Public Administration (ASPA) Code of Ethics.

## Why Ethics Belongs in This Discussion

Every promotion signals what an organization values. Rewarding seniority as a proxy for readiness, or confidence as a proxy for competence, teaches employees what to emulate. In public organizations, those signals must be measured against the paramount standard of the public interest. The choice of who leads is a high-stakes ethical act because it determines the moral integrity of the organization's authority, resource allocation, and relationship with the community.

The argument for ethical scrutiny is explicitly outlined in the ASPA Code of Ethics, which affirms eight core principles: advancing the public interest; upholding the Constitution and the law; promoting democratic participation; strengthening social equity; fully informing and advising; demonstrating personal integrity; promoting ethical organizations; and advancing professional excellence. A promotion that knowingly places an unprepared leader over staff—without training, mentoring, or support—risks violating several of these principles.

- **Violating the Duty to Prepare:** It misuses public resources, undermines integrity, and weakens organizational ethics. More critically, it neglects the ethical duty to inform, advise, and prepare both leaders and staff for success. The intentional withholding of training and mentorship is not merely an administrative oversight; it is a foreseeable failure that compromises the entire organization's ability to operate competently and uphold the law.
- **Violating Social Equity:** A lack of structured development, training, and transparent pathways exacerbates inequities. When promotion relies on informal networks (Chapter 4), opportunities are skewed, directly failing the ethical mandate to strengthen social equity. A merit system that is procedurally opaque reinforces existing power structures, meaning ethical failure disproportionately harms underrepresented talent and compromises the public mission's legitimacy.
- **Violating Public Trust:** An ethical organization (Chapter 8) must demonstrate competence. Promoting the unprepared compromises that demonstration, eroding the public's confidence in the institution's ability to steward resources and deliver services. The collective failure to ensure leader readiness transforms the organization's ethical stance from one of stewardship to one of indifference, damaging the essential currency of public service (Chapter 2).

The choice to promote is, therefore, a binding declaration of the organization's moral intent, carrying consequences that ripple through public morale and fiscal stability. These failures of preparation immediately implicate the leader's authority and the organization's fidelity to its public mission, requiring a clear understanding of the full scope of administrative responsibility.

# The Three Dimensions of Administrative Responsibility

Leadership promotions engage the full scope of administrative responsibility, which can be understood in three critical dimensions. Drawing on the foundational work of Harmon (1995), this triad clarifies the depth of the ethical commitment and the fiduciary nature of the management role:

## Responsibility as Agency

Responsibility as **Agency** defines the fundamental starting point: the organization possesses the **power to cause events to happen** through the voluntary exercise of its will, specifically in deciding who leads. This power to grant authority carries the immediate moral weight of choice—the organization consciously chooses to assume the risk of the leader's preparedness. Administrative responsibility begins here, at the moment discretion is exercised, as the organization serves as the agent of the public trust. The selection process itself, therefore, is not a neutral task but a declaration of moral intent, requiring the highest level of reasoned judgment to justify the action.

### Responsibility as Accountability

Responsibility as **Accountability** shifts the focus from the action to the consequences: the organization is formally entitled to be **answerable for foreseeable consequences**—the inevitable outcomes of its selection process. This dimension links the personnel decision directly to budgetary, safety, and operational costs (Chapter 2), making the failure to prepare a demonstrable breach of fiscal accountability. Historically, accountability has wrestled with the tension between strict obedience to external rules and the professional judgment of the administrator. However, the modern view recognizes that accountability must be mutual: the organization must be able to account for its discretion in selection, especially when technical training is prioritized over managerial readiness.

## Responsibility as Obligation

Responsibility as **Obligation** introduces a moral duty to act rightly, requiring the organization to minimize avoidable harm to staff and the public. This is the highest moral dimension, imposing the **Duty of Care** to staff and clients. This aligns with the necessity of acting in ways that are justified by morality and ethics, moving beyond mere procedural compliance. The commitment to ethical literacy and moral reasoning are essential to fulfilling this obligation. If an organization fails to ensure that its leaders demonstrate competence and integrity, it is violating this obligation, which the public has a right to expect from its public servants.

The challenge of Administrative Responsibility is precisely this ongoing struggle to link the procedural requirements of accountability with the subjective moral duty of obligation. Plant (2018) reinforces that administrative responsibility is the glue that connects administrative ethics to the broader questions of the proper role of unelected officials in a democratic system. The need for administrators to balance these competing demands—from political superiors, professional codes, and the public interest—is the enduring dilemma of the field.

Contemporary research confirms that this link between leadership and ethical performance is not merely theoretical, but empirical. Demir, Reddick, and Perlman (2023) found that organizational leadership not only promotes ethical behavior directly, but also indirectly through reinforcing the ethics culture in local governments. This demonstrates that the decision made in the Agency dimension—who to select as a leader—has a measurable, cascading effect on the Ethical Outcome (Obligation) of the entire organization. Therefore, the strategic design of the leadership pipeline is, in fact, an ethical technology that determines the moral performance of the public sector.

## Ethical Frameworks for Administrators

Ethical reasoning offers two primary orientations that public administrators must continuously balance. These orientations frame the fundamental conflict inherent in public service: the tension between upholding fair procedures and ensuring competent outcomes. Deciding who to promote requires honoring both dimensions of ethical responsibility, recognizing that an administrative action cannot be truly ethical if it sacrifices procedural justice for convenience, or if it prioritizes flawless procedure over predictable safety and outcome. This need to balance internal, rule-based standards with external, consequence-based demands is the enduring dilemma of the field.

## Duty-Based Reasoning (Deontology)

**Deontological** reasoning emphasizes adherence to obligations such as fairness, transparency, and due process. Rooted in the Greek word *deon* (meaning *duty*), this perspective judges an action's morality based on adherence to universal rules and principles, regardless of the ultimate consequences.

- **Foundation and Focus:** Deontology mandates that the public administrator adhere strictly to established professional standards and the spirit of the law. In promotion decisions, this means focusing rigorously on the fairness of the criteria, the transparency of the process (Chapter 6), and the duty to honor merit system structures. This commitment protects the system's integrity, ensuring that the process itself is just and visible to all citizens.
- **The Limitation:** While essential, a purely deontological approach is insufficient in public service because it could justify selecting an incompetent candidate simply because the *process was flawlessly executed* (e.g., the technical exam was fair). This outcome satisfies fairness but violates the *duty to prevent foreseeable harm* (a teleological concern).

## Consequence-Based Reasoning (Teleology)

**Teleological** reasoning stresses outcomes such as service quality, harm prevention, and public trust. Derived from the Greek word *telos* (meaning *goal, end, or purpose*), this orientation evaluates an action based on its ultimate result or benefit.

- **Foundation and Focus:** This perspective requires the administrator to anticipate the results of their decision, linking the choice directly to service quality and the overall mission. It demands selecting a candidate who is demonstrably competent and ready to lead, thereby

preventing the costly failure, staff burnout, and erosion of public confidence inherent in a poor promotion (Chapter 2).
- **The Ethical Imperative:** Teleology dictates that the administrator has an ethical obligation to ensure competence, treating the mitigation of foreseeable harm as a moral imperative that may occasionally outweigh strict adherence to rigid proceduralism, particularly if that proceduralism yields an ethically dangerous outcome.

The administrator cannot choose one over the other. Both a fair process is ethically necessary (deontology) and so is preventing foreseeable harm by ensuring competence (teleology). Classic texts such as Cooper's (*The Responsible Administrator*) and Lewis et al.'s (*The Ethics Challenge in Public Service*) highlight these dual obligations, showing how administrators must honor duty while also anticipating consequences. It aligns with Cooper's view that while morality assumes accepted modes of behavior rooted in formal rules and norms, ethics is "one step removed from action," relying on the careful examination and analysis of values and logic. Contemporary research reinforces that ethical leaders model fairness and foster climates where values and behavior align, producing measurable performance benefits. Put simply, how leaders are chosen and prepared profoundly affects service delivery and the public mission.

## When Promotions Become Ethical Failures

The systemic drivers of incompetence described earlier in this book (Chapters 3 and 4) each carry specific ethical weight. These drivers prove that administrative failures are not value-neutral; they are moral risks embedded within institutional design. When systems reward technical skill, longevity, or personal preference, they violate the merit principle and breach the public's implicit trust. This section analyzes the five major systemic factors—Merit System Myopia, Promotion from Within, Favoritism, Lack of Training, and De-emphasis of Education—and articulates precisely how each one translates the initial flaw in personnel management into an active, foreseeable ethical breach that causes measurable harm to the workforce and public service delivery.

- **Merit-system myopia:** When technical exams dominate selection, organizations can overlook demonstrable leadership readiness in supervision, budgeting, or conflict resolution. The duty to competence is not satisfied by technical filters alone.
- **Promotion from within:** Seniority can be good for morale and continuity, but when it substitutes for readiness, it becomes unfair to the team and to service recipients. Justice requires that opportunity be meaningful, not automatic.
- **Favoritism and personal preference:** Favoritism is not a "soft" problem. Research documents robust negative effects on performance and trust, including higher cynicism and knowledge-hiding behaviors that depress job performance (Arasli et al., 2020; Khalid et al., 2022). This behavioral response is an ethical injury to the workforce, destroying the psychological contract (Chapter 2). Favoritism distorts pipelines and can slide into politicized patronage dynamics, jeopardizing legitimacy (Kwon et al., 2021).
- **Lack of training and mentorship:** Placing someone in charge without preparation is a breach of the **duty of care** to the leader and to their team. It is foreseeable that untrained leaders will struggle with budgeting, supervision, or compliance (teleological failure). Prevention is an ethical obligation.
- **De-emphasis of public management education:** When organizations underinvest in management education, they compromise stewardship, inviting compliance failures or safety risks. This directly violates the fundamental premise of public administration: that its primary motive is service, not profit, and that its function is to provide essential goods to all citizens (Lewis et al., 2016).

**Practice Note: Favoritism as an Ethical Breach**

Favoritism violates integrity (privileging personal ties over fair criteria), undermines equity (skews opportunity), and weakens ethical culture (signals that process does not matter). In public agencies, it also jeopardizes legitimacy: citizens quickly infer that "who you know" matters more than competence. Transparent criteria, multiple assessors, and documented readiness evidence are essential ethical safeguards.

## Ethical Conflict and Ethical Congruence

Organizational ethics literature shows how "ethical conflicts" arise even in organizations that claim strong values. This conflict often stems from a breakdown between the organization's espoused values and its actual practices. When selection systems reward technical excellence but punish leaders for incompetence—or, conversely, when they reward favoritism but claim integrity—employees receive mixed, confusing, and contradictory ethical signals. When these systems send mixed signals or leaders behave inconsistently, employees retaliate or self-protect.

Navran (2002) described this in vivid terms as "feeding the hog" (rewarding misconduct or unethical behavior) or acting as "silent saboteurs" (internal resistance and cynicism). These are predictable behavioral responses to a perceived lack of fairness and a breakdown of trust within the organizational hierarchy.

The solution is ethical congruence: the comprehensive alignment of stated values, leader behavior, and organizational systems—both formal and informal. Formal systems include published codes, promotion policies, and reward structures; informal systems include leader modeling, peer norms, and the daily narratives of "how things really work". When congruence is missing, ethical conflict grows, leading to the high human and fiscal costs explored in Chapter 2. An ethics audit can reveal these gaps, showing precisely whether promotion practices truly match an organization's stated values and public mission.

## Practical Tests for Ethical Promotions

Principles and philosophical frameworks are essential for understanding why leadership misalignment is an ethical breach, but public administrators ultimately need decision tools to put ethics into practice. The core challenge of administrative ethics is honoring both the duty of fair process (deontology) and the responsibility for competent outcomes (teleology).

Navran (1996) proposed three "quick tests" for ethical congruence, which apply powerfully to promotion decisions, serving as a rapid, practical filter against potential bias, conflicts of interest, and the risk of manufactured incompetence. These tests are critical behavioral filters for bias:

- **The Butterfly Test: Does advancing this candidate—on this process, with this readiness evidence—give you ethical discomfort?** This test targets the administrator's internal subjective responsibility, forcing them to acknowledge the "gut feeling" of ethical tension. If the decision causes internal discomfort, it signals an unaddressed conflict (like favoritism or unmitigated risk) that must be identified and resolved before proceeding.
- **The Authority Test: Would you defend this promotion process and its rationale to a respected mentor, an ethics board, or the staff who will be led?** This shifts the focus to external accountability and professional standards. The administrator must ensure their reasoned elaboration of the decision—including the evidence of competence—is robust enough to withstand scrutiny from both professional peers and subordinates, verifying the commitment to integrity.
- **The Public Scrutiny Test: Would you be comfortable with the full process—criteria, interview notes, readiness evidence—on the front page of the newspaper?** This is the ultimate test of transparency and public trust (Chapter 2). If the administrator anticipates public condemnation for conflicts of interest or lack of due diligence, transparency is lacking, and the process must be revised to reflect the public interest.

A further test is alignment with the ASPA Code of Ethics. Would this promotion, if fully disclosed, advance the public interest, uphold the Constitution and the law, promote democratic participation, strengthen social equity, fully inform and advise, demonstrate personal integrity, promote ethical organizations, and advance professional excellence? If the answer is uncertain, the process has an ethical design problem, not just a management problem.

These philosophical and professional quick tests provide the essential ethical filter, but they require a structured administrative instrument for execution. To move from these high-level principles—such as Strengthening Social Equity and Advancing Professional Excellence—to objective verification, organizations need a detailed checklist that formalizes readiness criteria and transparency protocols. The following list provides a practical implementation tool for administrators to document their adherence to the full ethical mandate, ensuring all procedural and competency requirements are satisfied before final appointment.

> **Quick Check: Ethical Promotion Checklist**
> - Clear, job-relevant leadership competencies established in advance.
> - Multiple assessors and structured scoring that go beyond technical skills.
> - Transparent communication with candidates and affected teams.
> - Mentoring and development plans for selectees.
> - Equity review: Did outreach and criteria yield a fair slate, and are disparities addressed?
> - Three quick tests and ASPA alignment affirmatively satisfied.

## Responsibility, Stewardship, and Public Trust

Responsibility in administrative ethics is multifaceted. The choice of who leads is an act of Agency; the consequences of that choice require Accountability; and the moral imperative to ensure success constitutes the Obligation. Stewardship extends this duty forward. Leaders safeguard people, resources, and legitimacy. Ethical promotion practices are therefore acts of stewardship, ensuring that people, resources, and public trust are protected.

Research confirms that public leadership quality is consistently associated with better organizational outcomes (Backhaus & Vogel, 2022). In healthcare and other high-stakes environments, insufficiently prepared leaders increase risk, while leadership interventions improve performance (Al Khajeh, 2018).

## Case Illustrations

The ethical implications of promotion misalignment are starkest in practice. While the preceding sections provided the philosophical foundation and practical tests for ethical decisions, these real-world scenarios translate those concepts into tangible consequences for staff and public service delivery. These cases illustrate how the breakdown of administrative responsibility—whether due to lack of competence or due to favoritism—violates the public trust, and conversely, how intentional, ethically aligned processes can lead to measurable success.

**Case: The "Nice Fit" that Failed.**

A city department elevated a well-liked senior coordinator to division chief because "everyone liked working with him". There was no structured assessment of supervisory skill. Within six months, grievance filings rose, audit findings increased, and two high-performing analysts transferred out. A later review revealed that interview notes emphasized "fit" over readiness. A re-run using structured criteria, multiple assessors, and mentoring produced a stronger appointment.

*Ethical Checkpoint:* The Authority Test and the Public Scrutiny Test would have immediately flagged this promotion, forcing the department to justify prioritizing likability over documented leadership readiness. The ethical lesson is clear: favoritism breaches fairness and harms trust; transparent criteria and development plans are safeguards.

**Case: The Unprepared Clinical Lead.**

A clinically excellent nurse became unit manager without budgeting or scheduling training. Overtime spending grew, documentation lapses triggered safety concerns, and accreditation reviewers cited supervision gaps. After targeted training and peer coaching, budget variance decreased and safety metrics improved.

*Ethical Checkpoint:* This was a breach of the duty of care (deontological) because the harm was foreseeable. The lesson: duty of care requires preparing leaders before harm occurs; prevention is an ethical obligation.

**Case: Ethical Congruence in Practice.**

A county human services agency rebuilt its promotion process around explicit competencies, structured panels, and a mentorship pipeline. Scoring rubrics were published, and unsuccessful candidates received development feedback tied to learning plans. Internal survey scores on "fair promotion process" rose, turnover decreased, and audit variances declined.

*Ethical Checkpoint*: This case demonstrates that ethical congruence—alignment of values, behavior, and systems—produces measurable trust and performance gains. The process upheld the principles of transparency, equity, and professional excellence.

## Ethical Imperative Going Forward

Promotions into incompetence are not random failures. They are manufactured when systems reward the wrong signals and ignore foreseeable risks. Ethical frameworks clarify what is at stake: fairness, competence, stewardship, and public trust.

The imperative is simple to state and difficult to do: design fair processes, require readiness evidence, invest in preparation, and hold leaders accountable for modeling the values the organization claims. Ethical congruence ensures that "leadership is learned, not assumed" is not just a phrase but a professional standard.

## Conclusion

The ASPA Code of Ethics reminds administrators to advance the public interest, uphold the Constitution and the law, promote participation, strengthen equity, provide honest advice, demonstrate integrity, promote ethical organizations, and advance professional excellence. This final analytical chapter has established that the solutions presented throughout the book—from pipeline design (Chapter 6) to collective competence (Chapter 8)—are not merely management strategies; they are acts of ethical governance.

The full portfolio of solutions provided in this book—including the Leadership Alignment Project (Appendix B) and its templates (Appendix C)—

serves as a practical guide for implementing this ethical imperative, ensuring that organizations make competence the ethical foundation of every promotion decision. Chapter 10 unites these ethical and systemic lessons into a framework for institutionalizing competence as a core public value.

# Chapter 10 – Synthesis and Call to Action

Competent leadership is not accidental—it is cultivated, sustained, and shared.

## Reconnecting the Threads

Across this book, we traced a paradox hiding in plain sight: organizations routinely reward technical mastery with promotion, then demand a wholly different craft — leading people, stewarding systems, and building trust — without providing the requisite preparation. The result is a pattern of manufactured misalignment: leaders selected for past performance are held accountable for future responsibilities they were never taught to shoulder. The organizational whiplash that follows is predictable —and preventable.

Chapters 1 and 2 established the trap and its costs. Chapters 3 and 4 surfaced systemic drivers: civil-service qualifiers that overweight technical screens, promotion norms that default to seniority, favoritism that bypasses readiness, developmental gaps that leave new managers to "figure it out," and educational pipelines that under-emphasize the practice of management. Chapters 5 through 8 shifted the lens from diagnosis to design—how to define leadership readiness, build intentional pipelines, equip emerging leaders, and transition from solo excellence to collective leadership. Chapter 9 anchored the work in ethics: promoting without preparation is not only inefficient; it breaches a **duty of care** to employees and the public. As Plant (2018) reminds us, **administrative responsibility** is the connective tissue between ethical governance and democratic legitimacy—the perpetual balancing act between *external accountability* and *internal moral reasoning*. Competence is therefore not only technical alignment, but also moral discernment exercised within public trust.

This chapter weaves those threads into a single fabric. It offers a practical, research-informed framework for building competent leadership as an institutional resource rather than a personal accident; translates that framework into commitments for institutions and practitioners; and closes with a moral and civic imperative: competence is the pathway by which public organizations earn and sustain trust (Heifetz & Linsky, 2017)

## The Integrated Leadership Confidence Framework

Leadership competence is sustained where **three domains overlap** —it is an outcome achieved only when organizational structure, personal development, and ethical fidelity reinforce one another. This framework provides the unifying model for the entire book, moving the discussion from identifying isolated failures (Chapters 3 and 4) to engineering resilient capacity (Chapter 6). This holistic perspective demands that organizations consciously manage competence as a systemic asset, recognizing that deficiency in any one area will compromise the strength of the other two. The three domains that must be aligned to sustain ethical competence are:

- **Systemic** – This domain addresses the organizational architecture of competence, focusing on *how people are selected and supported*. It requires dismantling the old patronage and merit structures (Chapter 3) and replacing them with objective, transparent pipelines that ensure accountability flows between HR and line leadership.
- **Developmental** – This domain governs capability continuity, focusing on *how capabilities are built and reinforced*. It mandates the shift from episodic, event-based training to multimodal development (Chapter 4), where experiential learning, coaching, and psychological safety reinforce behavioral transfer.
- **Ethical** – This domain establishes the moral governance of the system, focusing on *how stewardship and equity govern decisions and behavior*. It ensures that the selection process upholds the duty of care and that the pursuit of efficiency does not compromise social equity or public trust (Chapter 9).

Treating any one domain in isolation invites relapse; treating all three creates a durable, renewable capacity for competent leadership. The framework is both diagnostic and design-oriented. It recognizes that competence is not a trait but a systemic outcome—the product of decisions about who is promoted, how they are prepared, and what values govern the journey.

This intellectual synthesis demonstrates that the solution to *promoted into incompetence* is not a single fix, but a deliberate commitment to aligning policy with morality. The following visualization, Table 10.1, presents this framework, detailing how the root causes of misalignment across the three domains must be met with specific enablers and sustaining conditions to build capacity that lasts.

*Table 10.1 – Leadership Competence Framework*
*(Systemic • Developmental • Ethical)*

| Domain | Root Causes (Why we get misalignment) | Enablers (How we fix selection & growth) | Sustaining Conditions (How we make it stick) |
|---|---|---|---|
| Systemic | Technical qualifiers over readiness; seniority default; favoritism exceptions; fragmented accountability | Role-anchored competency profiles; structured comparative selection; transparent mobility criteria; pipeline ownership shared by HR + line leadership | Routine validity checks; internal-mobility dashboards; leader performance tied to people & service outcomes |
| Developmental | "Sink-or-swim" promotions; training without transfer; episodic programs | Blended development (coaching + feedback + stretch assignments); line-manager | Learning climate with psychological safety (Edmondson, 2018); protected practice time; |

| | | | |
|---|---|---|---|
| | | involvement; evaluation beyond smile sheets (Kirkpatrick & Kirkpatrick, 2016) | integration with performance management |
| Ethical | Duty of care unarticulated; equity impacts ignored; tolerance of soft favoritism | Explicit duty-of-care policy; ethics code applied to promotion & mentoring (ASPA, n.d.); bias-aware panels & documentation | Regular ethics/equity audits; transparent remedies; leader accountability for fair development access (Demir et al., 2023; Svara, 2014; Plant, 2018) |

The table successfully synthesizes the framework. Implementing this comprehensive framework from conceptual alignment to operational reality is the defining charge for leadership in public, healthcare, and nonprofit organizations. The enduring question is not whether the system *can* be fixed, but whether the institution has the moral courage and political will to enforce the necessary changes in culture, measurement, and resource allocation. The failure to adopt this holistic approach guarantees the perpetuation of the *readiness gap* and the continuous payment of *managerial tuition*.

## Translating the Framework into Action – The Institutional Imperative

Institutions create competence when they engineer it on purpose. The institutional imperative requires a conscious repudiation of old, high-risk practices and the deliberate installation of low-risk, high-return systems. This structural commitment transforms the organization from one that punishes failure into one that proactively prevents it, protecting public resources and enhancing service quality. To achieve this shift from accidental readiness to engineered competence, three fundamental changes must be enforced across the organizational infrastructure:

- **From tasks to behaviors.** Redefine roles by observable behaviors (e.g., facilitates performance conversations, manages variance, builds coalitions). The traditional reliance on technical task mastery (Chapter 3) must be replaced by a focus on the demonstrated behavioral competencies of leading people and managing ambiguity (Chapter 5). This ensures that the criteria for promotion align precisely with the *work* the new leader will actually perform.
- **From programs to transfer.** Workshops alone rarely change behavior; blend coaching, feedback, and stretch assignments with real-world evaluation. Developmental investment must target behavioral transfer, verifying that learned skills are consistently applied on the job. Without rigorous evaluation of behavioral change (Level 3) and organizational impact (Level 4), training remains merely an expense, not a strategic capability builder.
- **From discretionary mentoring to accountable pipelines.** Pipelines require co-ownership by HR and line leaders, equitable access, and transparent readiness criteria. This systemic accountability removes the bias inherent in discretionary mentoring and favoritism (Chapter 3) by formalizing the structure that guides and tracks high-potential talent. When pipeline ownership is shared, capacity management becomes a collective responsibility, securing capability continuity against the certainty of turnover.

The development of organizational ethics cannot rely on goodwill alone. As Svara (2014) observes, sustaining ethical behavior requires institutional architecture—codes, training, and enforcement mechanisms that turn aspirations into standards. ASPA's Code of Ethics serves as a "keeper of the code," linking personal conscience with collective accountability. Competent institutions likewise codify what ethical leadership looks like, teach it explicitly, and measure adherence to it.

**Practice Note 10.1 — Institutional Commitments for Competence**

- **Publish the profile.** Define behavioral standards for each supervisory tier.
- **Tie selection to profile.** Use structured interviews and work samples.
- **Guarantee onboarding.** Provide a 90-day mentorship and practice plan.
- **Evaluate transfer.** Measure on-the-job behavior change, not attendance.

## The Individual Imperative – A Practitioner's Checklist

Systems matter, but agency lives with leaders. The transition from "expert" to "enabler" demands new muscles: self-regulation, situational judgment, and the ability to deliver results through others. This intentional self-development is the necessary counterpart to the organizational commitment defined in the pipeline. The leader's readiness journey ultimately rests on their ability to cultivate a Growth Mindset and adopt habits that actively challenge their comfort zone. Habits that accelerate readiness include curiosity over certainty, capacity-building over control, and learning from evidence rather than defending expertise. This commitment transforms individual effort into a sustained capability that mitigates the systemic risks identified throughout the book.

> **Quick Check 10.1 — Am I Ready to Lead Competently?**
> - The following checklist serves as a continuous self-audit, shifting the focus from simply reporting on tasks completed to evaluating demonstrable leadership behaviors (Level 3 of the Kirkpatrick Model, Chapter 6). A "no" answer is not failure; it is a development plan. Competence grows where leaders treat feedback as fuel.
> - **Have I helped a direct report grow two observable behaviors in the last 60 days?** This diagnostic question measures Coaching and Capacity-Building—the core task of an "enabler." A positive answer confirms that the leader is dedicating time to team development (ECQ: Leading People) and successfully transferring knowledge, directly countering the micro-management trap.
> - **Have I run a difficult performance conversation with follow-up documentation?** This measures Emotional Competence and Accountability—the leader's willingness to engage in candid, high-

stakes communication. This act requires self-regulation (Chapter 7) and establishes the procedural justice necessary to manage staff performance fairly, countering the Culture of Silence (Chapter 1).

- **Can I explain this quarter's budget variances and the trade-offs I made?** This measures Fiscal Stewardship and Strategic Judgment—the shift from technical accuracy to business acumen. This skill (ECQ: Business Acumen) demonstrates the ability to link financial data to strategic policy choices and manage resources responsibly, fulfilling a core ethical duty (Chapter 9).

- **Have I built one cross-unit coalition and shared lessons learned?** This measures Systems Thinking and Coalition Building—the capacity to influence across organizational boundaries (ECQ: Building Coalitions). Successfully building coalitions proves the leader can navigate the interdependence required of modern public service, mitigating departmental silo risks.

A "no" answer is not failure; it is a development plan. Competence grows where leaders treat feedback as fuel. This constant self-audit, performed with honesty and intention, is the single greatest defense against the confidence-competence gap. By institutionalizing these habits of self-diagnosis, the emerging leader fulfills their personal duty, making their development not a passive request but a measurable, strategic commitment that demands reciprocal support from the organization's external systems.

## The Policy and Educational Imperative

Public administration does not happen in a vacuum. Civil-service rules, accreditation norms, and university curricula function as powerful external forces that collectively define what constitutes competence, often dictating what is measured, taught, and rewarded in public and nonprofit service. If these external systems remain anchored in outdated models that prioritize technical knowledge and passive compliance, organizational efforts to build pipelines (Chapter 6) will be continuously undermined. Therefore, addressing the manufactured incompetence trap requires concurrent reform targeting these foundational external structures:

- **Civil-service modernization:** Selection tools must test for leadership behavior, not just technical knowledge. This is a direct imperative to update the foundational merit systems (Chapter 3) by replacing general, low-predictive technical exams with structured interviews, work samples, and simulations that assess core leadership competencies (e.g., conflict management, strategic judgment, delegation). Policy reform must explicitly align the hiring mandate with the behavioral demands of the job, removing bureaucratic hurdles that prioritize tenure over verified readiness.
- **Accreditation and continuing education:** Standards should require practice-based management, ethics, and cross-boundary collaboration. Accreditation bodies (for MPA, MPH, and MS-HCA programs) must use their influence to close the curriculum-to-practice bridge, mandating that graduate education emphasizes the "how" of public management—fiscal stewardship, supervision, and governance ethics (Chapter 4)—alongside the "why" of policy analysis. This ensures that professionals enter the workforce equipped with functional managerial skills.
- **Universities as partners:** MPA and MS-HCA programs can close the curriculum-to-practice bridge through real-client capstones and practitioner co-teaching. The research confirms that public administration struggles when the academic core shifts away from teaching the "how" of public management, emphasizing the need for intentional partnership to rebuild essential competency in ethics and resource stewardship.

Policy reform is not about adding hurdles; it is about selecting for what the job truly requires and teaching to the work leaders actually do. The implementation of these structural and educational reforms addresses the technical challenge of competence. However, competence is merely the mechanism; the ultimate motivation for these massive institutional changes must be ethical. Moving beyond procedural fixes requires confronting the reality that leadership failure carries devastating human and civic consequences. Therefore, the implementation of these policy changes is inseparable from the final, highest obligation of public service—the Moral Imperative to protect the public trust through sustained, ethical stewardship.

## The Moral Imperative – Stewardship and Trust

Competence carries an ethical charge. Organizations owe new leaders preparation proportionate to the responsibility they confer; leaders owe their teams and communities a commitment to develop capacities they do not yet possess. Failing either side imposes tangible human and fiscal costs. As Cooper (2006) and Plant (2018) assert, leadership is an act of stewardship over public resources and legitimacy, meaning the failure to prepare is inherently a moral failure, not just an administrative error.

Recent empirical evidence reinforces this view, demonstrating that leadership competence is the necessary catalyst for organizational ethical performance. Demir, Reddick, and Perlman (2023) found that ethical leadership exerts both a direct influence on ethical performance and an indirect one through the reinforcement of ethical culture. Leadership ethics are contagious: when leaders model and institutionalize ethical norms, culture becomes the conduit and leadership the catalyst for sustained ethical performance.

Three complementary duties follow from this imperative:

- **Duty of care to the leader.** Promotion without preparation is institutional negligence. Designing readiness honors those elevated by mitigating the risk of foreseeable harm and preventing the personal anxiety and distress of the confidence-competence gap (Chapter 1).
- **Duty to the workforce.** Employees have a right to competent supervision—the scaffolding for safety and growth. Unprepared leadership creates moral injury and burnout (Chapter 2), making the commitment to a ready leader a necessary investment in the team's professional health and safety.
- **Duty to the public.** Public trust is not a practice field; competence is equity, protecting those least able to absorb failure. When a service fails due to unprepared management, the harm falls disproportionately on vulnerable communities that rely most heavily

on public and nonprofit services, violating the mandate of social equity (Chapter 9).

Leadership development, framed this way, is not a perk but a justice project—paying tuition for leadership up front so the public does not pay later in failure, waste, or cynicism. This commitment transforms the administrative act of personnel development into an essential civic function. By prioritizing equitable selection, comprehensive readiness, and sustained competence, the organization ensures that the Duty of Care is fully met. This proactive investment in ethical leadership is the single most powerful way public organizations can rebuild and sustain the public trust on which democratic legitimacy depends, finally converting the risk of manufactured incompetence into the promise of systemic, collective competence.

## Conclusion – Leadership as a Renewable Resource

The opposite of *promoted into incompetence* is not perfection; it is a system that engineers competence—where ethical selection, mentored onboarding, deliberate practice, and stewardship reinforce one another until they become culture.

This is the charge of the book: **design what you value.** If you value competent leadership, make it visible, teachable, measurable, and shared. Publish the profile. Select against it. Onboard to it. Coach within it. Evaluate transfer, not attendance. Audit fairness, not intention. Hold leaders accountable for building capacity, not hoarding expertise.

### The Call to Action: Your Ethical Imperative

The failures detailed in this book—the ethical breaches, the lost trust, the managerial tuition—are not an inevitable fate; they are the consequence of deferred decision. The time for passive leadership is over. You now possess the framework to identify systemic flaws (Chapter 3) and the tools to enforce structural integrity (Chapter 6). This is your ethical imperative:

- **For Institutions:** Refuse to promote potential into paralysis. Invest in development as infrastructure, not as an afterthought. Institutionalize

the principles of ethical congruence (Chapter 9) so that your practices consistently reflect your public mandate.
- **For Practitioners:** Reject the Readiness Illusion (Chapter 1). Own your development, seek candid feedback, and commit to the deliberate practice (Chapter 7) that scales personal mastery into public value. Be the leader who models vulnerability and actively creates psychological safety (Chapter 8).

Competent leadership is not accidental; it is cultivated, sustained, and shared. When institutions make that choice — systemically, developmentally, and ethically — they convert individual excellence into public value and rebuild the trust on which democratic life depends. Competent leadership is not accidental. The health of our public, healthcare, and nonprofit sectors depends on your courage to implement this change now.

# Glossary

This glossary defines key terms, frameworks, and concepts introduced throughout *Promoted into Incompetence.* Each entry reflects how the term is applied within the context of public service, healthcare, and nonprofit leadership practice. Cross-references and chapter citations are included to guide deeper study and classroom discussion. Together, these definitions provide a shared language for understanding competence, ethics, and readiness in leadership.

**Accountability** — The administrative obligation for an organization or leader to be answerable for the predictable outcomes and consequences of their actions or decisions, especially those concerning resource stewardship and personnel selection (Ch. 9). *See also: Responsibility as Obligation, Ethical Stewardship*

**Adaptive Work** — Leadership activity focused on mobilizing people to tackle complex, systemic problems that require changing ingrained beliefs, values, and norms, rather than just applying technical fixes). Adaptive work inherently generates resistance and conflict. *Application: Contrasts with technical work, which solves definable problems* (Ch. 1).

**Administrative Responsibility** — The glue that connects administrative ethics to the questions regarding the proper role and behavior of unelected officials in a democratic system. It is the ongoing challenge of linking procedural accountability with moral reasoning (Ch. 9). *See also: Agency, Accountability, Obligation*

**Agency** — The fundamental dimension of administrative responsibility defining an organization's moral and legal power to cause events to happen through the voluntary exercise of choice, particularly in delegating authority (Ch. 9). *See also: Responsibility as Accountability, Responsibility as Obligation*

**After-Action Review (AAR)** — A mandatory, disciplined reflection process, originally military, conducted immediately after an event (successful or failed) to diagnose process flaws rather than assign individual blame. The AAR transforms experience into collective intelligence (Ch. 8). *See also: Psychological Safety, Collective Competence*

**ASPA Code of Ethics** — The set of eight core principles established by the American Society for Public Administration (ASPA) that provides the professional ethical standard for public administrators. The Code must be applied to promotion decisions to ensure ethical governance (Ch. 9).

**Backlog Aging** — A key leading indicator of operational failure, measuring the average time old, unresolved service cases or administrative tasks have been awaiting action. A sharp spike signals poor workload management and impending leadership misalignment (Ch. 2).

**Bureaucratic Features** — Characteristics of a rigid civil service system, such as excessive rules, slowness, and a lack of accountability. These features often become intricately commingled with the original ideal of Merit (Ch. 3).

**Behavioral Competencies** — Measurable, observable leadership skills (e.g., delegation, conflict management, fiscal stewardship) that demonstrate prospective capability, distinct from technical knowledge (Ch. 5). Used in structured interviews to gauge leadership readiness (Ch. 3). *See also: Readiness Indicators*

**Burnout** — The chronic erosion of the relationship between people and their work, typically manifesting as exhaustion, cynicism, and reduced professional efficacy. It is a frequent human cost of working under misaligned, unprepared leadership (Ch. 2). *See also: Moral Injury*

**Candor Gap** — The difficulty experienced by newly promoted internal leaders (Factor 2) in providing honest, critical feedback or enforcing accountability with former colleagues and peers. This compromises managerial effectiveness (Ch. 3). *Application: Addressed through mentorship and external coaching* (Ch. 4).

**Capability Continuity** — The focus of pipeline thinking, asking "What essential competencies and functions must endure regardless of who sits here?" It contrasts with traditional succession planning, which focuses only on replacement (Ch. 6). *See also: Leadership Pipeline*

**Collective Competence** — A systemic capability achieved when teams move beyond individual contribution to shared habits of trust, reflection, and coordinated action. This is ethical competence writ large and the final organizational defense against manufactured incompetence (Ch. 8).

**Competence vs. Readiness Matrix** — A diagnostic tool (Template 4) used to map candidates against two distinct axes: technical competence (what they know) and leadership readiness (what they can do through others). Used to formalize the decision process and prevent subjective promotions. Application: Guides the strategy for promotion ("Promote Now") or development ("Delay + Develop") (Ch. 3).

**Competency Inflation** — The administrative failure of relying on long lists of desirable leadership traits that lack precise operational definitions and measurable standards. This renders the list useless for training or objective selection (Ch. 4).

**Confidence–Competence Gap** — The core psychological flaw where an individual's confidence in their ability to lead (often based on technical mastery) outpaces their actual managerial competence. This gap is exacerbated by the Readiness Illusion (Ch. 1).

**Cronyism** — A form of favoritism rooted in conferring advantages based on personal relationships, loyalty, or shared networks rather than objective competence. This practice is an ethical breach that destabilizes organizational credibility (Ch. 3). *See also: Upward Managing*

**Culture of Silence** — The pervasive organizational habit of withholding critical information, dissent, or errors out of fear of punishment or retribution

(Ch. 1). It is the opposite of psychological safety and is a primary enabler of manufactured incompetence (Ch. 8).

**Curriculum-to-Practice Bridge** — An imperative for educational institutions and agencies to align graduate curricula (MPA, MS-HCA) with the practical management, ethics, and supervision skills required on the job. Application: Achieved through capstone residencies and practitioner co-teaching (Ch. 4).

**Deontology** — A duty-based ethical framework emphasizing adherence to universal moral obligations, such as fairness, transparency, and due process. In promotions, it requires a just *process*, regardless of the outcome's competence (Ch. 9). See also: Teleology

**Developmental Deficits** — The sins of omission (Factor 4 and 5) where organizations fail to provide necessary preparation, training, or mentorship to new leaders. These deficits magnify structural flaws and guarantee a difficult transition (Ch. 4).

**Distributed Leadership** — A concept acknowledging that leadership capacity is not confined to a single positional leader but is a collective property of a team or organization. It emphasizes shared accountability and coordinated action (Ch. 8). See also: Collective Competence, Leadership Capacity

**Dunning–Kruger Effect** — The psychological phenomenon where individuals with low competence overestimate their abilities because their incompetence robs them of the metacognitive ability to recognize their deficits (Ch. 1).

**Duty of Care** — The core moral obligation to minimize avoidable harm, specifically applied to promotion by requiring that the organization provide newly elevated leaders with the training and support necessary to succeed. Neglect of this duty is institutional negligence (Ch. 9). See also: Ethical Stewardship, Responsibility as Obligation

**ECQs (Executive Core Qualifications)** — The five clusters of leadership competencies defined by the U.S. OPM for executive leadership: Leading

Change, Leading People, Results Driven, Business Acumen, and Building Coalitions. They provide a non-technical framework for measuring readiness (Ch. 3).

**Emotional Competence (EQ)** — The capacity to manage one's own emotions and those of others, comprising self-awareness, self-regulation, and empathy. It is the non-negotiable core for effective leadership, transforming raw authority into influence (Ch. 7).

**Ethical Congruence** — The state achieved when an organization's stated values (codes, mission), leader behavior (modeling), and formal systems (promotion policies) are comprehensively aligned. Congruence counters cynicism and promotes measurable trust (Ch. 9).

**Ethical Stewardship** — The practice of leaders managing their authority, influence, and public resources responsibly in service of the common good. It is a core duty that mandates preventive investment in leader preparation (Ch. 9). *See also: Duty of Care, Stewardship*

**Ethical Vigilance** — A systemic competence where a team or organization actively monitors and corrects ethical boundaries, viewing challenging a poor decision as a loyal act of system protection. This requires moral courage to flourish (Ch. 8).

**Favoritism** — A systemic driver of incompetence (Factor 3) where appointments are made based on personal preference, loyalty, or comfort rather than objective competence or merit. It is an ethical breach that violates fairness (Ch. 9). *See also: Cronyism, Upward Managing*

**Fiduciary Duty** — The legal and ethical requirement to manage resources and influence responsibly on behalf of a public or client interest. Measuring pipeline health is considered a fiduciary duty (Ch. 6).

**Fiscal Stewardship** — A core leadership competency (ECQ: Business Acumen) requiring strategic risk management and the use of financial data to justify mission choices, rather than simply maintaining budgetary accuracy (Ch. 5).

**Growth Mindset** — The psychological belief (Dweck, 2006) that one's abilities and intelligence are not fixed traits but can be developed through effort, dedication, and learning from setbacks. Essential for overcoming identity dissonance (Ch. 7).

**Identity Dissonance** — The profound emotional and psychological adjustment required when a technical expert transitions to a leader, where their worth is no longer measured by personal output but by the competence and growth of others (Ch. 5).

**Innovation Frequency** — A leading indicator of collective readiness, measuring the team's capacity for adaptive work by tracking the number of small experiments or non-traditional solutions initiated (Ch. 8).

**Justice Project** — The ethical imperative to frame leadership development as a matter of social equity, ensuring preparation is provided up front so vulnerable populations (the public) do not pay the cost of failure later (Ch. 10).

**Kirkpatrick Model** — The most widely adopted framework for training evaluation, identifying four levels of assessment: Reaction (Level 1), Learning (Level 2), Behavior (Level 3), and Results (Level 4). Public organizations must strive for Levels 3 and 4 (Ch. 6).

**Lagging Indicators** — Measurable consequences that reflect damage already incurred by the organization, such as high turnover rates, budget variance, or increased audit findings. They prove the cost of misalignment (Ch. 2). *See also: Leading Indicators*

**Leading Indicators** — Early, observable behavioral and operational warnings that predict future crises before costs fully accumulate. Used to shift from reactive damage control to proactive coaching (Ch. 2). *See also: Lagging Indicators*

**Leadership Alignment Project** — The eight-week, field-based capstone exercise (Appendix B) designed for emerging leaders to observe a real organization, diagnose misalignment drivers, and design practical interventions (App. B).

**Leadership Drainers** — Untrained managers who prioritize their own control and output, consuming team time and energy by micromanaging, ultimately resulting in high turnover and low engagement (Ch. 5).

**Leadership Pipeline** — The deliberate **infrastructure** that moves potential leaders from technical mastery to strategic stewardship through four working chambers: Identification, Preparation, Transition Support, and Renewal. It treats competence as a managed asset class (Ch. 6).

**Leadership Readiness** — The measurable behavioral competence to lead people, steward systems, and navigate ambiguity. It is a state that must be cultivated and measured, not assumed (Ch. 5). *See also: Readiness Gap*

**Learning Agility** — The core competency of adaptive leadership: the ability to learn quickly from new experiences and apply that learning to novel situations. It fuels a leader's adaptation to the demands of a new role (Ch. 7).

**Learning Loops** — The iterative process by which leadership growth occurs: exposure → application → feedback → reflection. These must be institutionalized rather than left to personal luck (Ch. 6). *See also: Multimodal Development*

**Managerial Tuition** — The high, non-recuperable cost an organization pays for unchecked leadership misalignment, usually appearing *after* a promotion as turnover, rework, lost productivity, low morale, and reputational damage. It is the price of learning by failure (Ch. 2).

**Manufactured Incompetence** — A systemic organizational failure where leadership deficiency is created not by a lack of individual ability, but by the intentional lack of preparation, flawed selection systems, and developmental neglect. This is a predictable, structural misalignment (Ch. 1).

**Merit Principle** — The ethical ideal that public employment and promotion should be based on competence, qualifications, and the absence of political favoritism (Ch. 3). When corrupted by factors like seniority or favoritism, it is said to be violated (Ch. 9).

**Merit System Myopia** — A systemic driver (Factor 1) where selection processes (like civil service exams) overvalue technical skills and retrospective compliance, resulting in a failure to measure or select for essential leadership competencies like fiscal stewardship or conflict management (Ch. 3).

**Moral Courage** — The willingness to stand up for core ethical values and challenge ethical slippage or systemic failures despite the risk of personal cost. It requires psychological safety to flourish (Ch. 8).

**Moral Injury** — The deep psychological distress that arises when an individual's work violates their personal or professional values, often due to systemic failures or unethical managerial behavior. It is a frequent human cost of misaligned leadership (Ch. 2). *See also: Burnout*

**Multimodal Development** — A strategic approach to building leadership competence that moves beyond isolated training events to integrate multiple, reinforcing methods—including formal instruction, coaching, multisource feedback, and structured stretch assignments. This maximizes the transfer of learning (Ch. 4).

**Non-Linear Competence** — The managerial capability required at strategic and enterprise levels that involves navigating ambiguity, synthesizing disparate information, and aligning political objectives with ethical duty. It contrasts with the simpler linear focus of technical work (Ch. 6).

**Obligation** — The highest dimension of administrative responsibility, defining the moral duty to act rightly and minimize avoidable harm to staff and the public. Fulfilling this requires competence and ethical literacy (Ch. 9). *See also: Duty of Care*

**Organizational Dependency** — A failure pattern where unprepared managers who struggle with delegation unintentionally train their teams to wait for specific, micro-level instructions. This fosters learned helplessness (Ch. 2).

**Peer-to-Boss Transition** — The perilous shift in professional identity for an internal promotion (Factor 2), requiring the leader to move from peer advocacy to managerial accountability. Often results in the Candor Gap (Ch. 3).

**Performance-Potential Fallacy** — The false assumption that the behaviors that predict success as an individual contributor (technical skill, adherence to process) are sufficient or predictive for success in management roles (Ch. 1).

**Personal Development Plan (PDP)** — A formal, personalized blueprint created by the individual leader that links their aspirations to the organization's competencies, specifying *what* skills they will acquire, *how* they will practice them, and *who* will provide coaching (Ch. 7).

**Peter Principle** — The observation that people tend to rise to their "level of incompetence" because promotions rely more on retrospective performance (success in the past job) than prospective capability (readiness for the new job) (Ch. 1).

**Principled Dissent** — The act of constructively challenging existing organizational assumptions or perceived flaws (often unethical or systemic) out of commitment to the public mission (Ch. 7). It requires a culture of Psychological Safety to be effectively utilized (Ch. 8).

**Procedural Justice** — An ethical practice ensuring fairness, transparency, and consistency in daily decision-making (e.g., performance reviews, resource allocation). Its absence fuels cynicism (Ch. 9).

**Prospective Capability** — The forward-looking evaluation metric that assesses a candidate's potential to succeed in a future role, based on observable behaviors and readiness indicators, rather than relying solely on past performance (Ch. 3). *Application: The direct counterpoint to Retrospective Performance (Ch. 1).*

**Prohibited Personnel Practices (PPPs)** — Specific legal violations in U.S. federal practice that guard against favoritism and nepotism. Favoritism is considered a reportable legal violation (Ch. 3).

**Psychological Capital** — The emotional, mental, and social resources leaders and teams use to sustain performance, which can be depleted by misalignment. Includes concepts like Moral Courage and Self-Efficacy (Ch. 7).

**Psychological Contract** — The unwritten expectations between an employer and employee (Rousseau, 1995). This contract is ruptured when promotions are based on favoritism or unreadiness (Ch. 2).

**Psychological Safety** — The shared belief among team members that the environment is safe for interpersonal risk-taking, such as admitting a mistake or engaging in principled dissent, without fear of punishment or humiliation. It is the foundation for collective learning (Ch. 8). *See also: Culture of Silence*

**Readiness Illusion** — The psychological trap where high performers internalize praise and confidence as proof of leadership readiness, resulting in a belief that prior technical achievement guarantees future managerial success (Ch. 1).

**Readiness Ratio** — A core metric for pipeline health, tracking the percentage of key supervisory or strategic roles that have at least one identified and actively prepared successor. It measures vulnerability to unexpected turnover (Ch. 6).

**Reflection-in-Action** — The practice of pausing briefly *within* the workflow to ask what is being learned, rather than waiting until the task is complete

(Ch. 8). This embeds learning more deeply than classroom exposure alone (Ch. 6). *See also: Learning Loops*

**Renewable Resource** — The concept of viewing competence not as a finite resource tied to individuals, but as an asset that can be tracked, sustained, and perpetually renewed through intentional pipeline infrastructure (Ch. 6).

**Rework Reduction Rate** — A Level 4 Result metric demonstrating impact by measuring the reduction in preventable errors, corrections, or excess overtime caused by leadership failure. This directly proves cost recovery (Ch. 8).

**Right-First-Time Percentage** — A key performance indicator (KPI) measuring the ratio of work completed successfully without requiring significant rework or error correction. It is a direct indicator of operational effectiveness under leadership (Ch. 2).

**Selective Attrition Pattern** — The negative organizational consequence where misalignment causes high-performing, often underrepresented, employees to transfer out or exit, thereby weakening diversity and institutional competence (Ch. 2).

**Self-Efficacy** — An individual's belief in their own capability to execute the actions necessary to manage prospective situations successfully (Bandura, 1997). A key psychological multiplier for overcoming identity dissonance (Ch. 7).

**Self-Regulation** — An essential component of Emotional Competence involving the capacity to manage stress, impulses, and negative emotional reactions, especially when facing high-stakes conflict. Its absence leads to toxic micromanagement (Ch. 7).

**Seniority Trap** — A systemic driver (Factor 2) where internal promotion defaults to longevity or time served as a proxy for leadership readiness, risking the prioritization of familiarity over true capability (Ch. 3).

**Sins of Omission** — The two systemic failures (Factor 4 and 5) explored in Chapter 4 where organizations fail to provide necessary management training, mentorship, or education to the leaders they promote (Ch. 4).

**Social Equity** — The ethical mandate to treat all persons with fairness, justice, and equality, actively working to reduce disparities in outcomes and increase the inclusion of underrepresented groups (Ch. 9). It is the core of the Justice Project (Ch. 10).

**Sponsors** — Key roles in an individual's developmental network who use their positional influence to create opportunities for advancement and visibility, often securing stretch assignments (Ch. 7).

**Systems Thinking** — A core Cognitive Competency of emotional intelligence that enables a leader to see connections between policy, resources, and public outcomes, moving beyond piece-meal fixes to holistic solutions for complex challenges (Ch. 5).

**Stewardship** — The core ethical principle requiring leaders to manage their authority, influence, and public resources responsibly in service of the common good (Ch. 9). It contrasts with the mindset of personal control (Ch. 8). *See also: Ethical Stewardship*

**Strategic Statement** — The leader's view of the budget, which sees it as a document connecting organizational values to long-term outcomes and mission priorities, contrasting with the technical expert's view of it as a mere compliance document (Ch. 5).

**Structured Behavioral Interview** — A multi-method assessment technique used for selection, requiring candidates to provide specific examples of past behavior (STAR format) that are scored against validated leadership competencies (Ch. 3).

**Structured Stretch Assignment** — A developmental tool where emerging leaders are intentionally placed in high-visibility, high-learning roles (e.g., leading a cross-agency capstone) to exercise competencies before receiving the formal promotion title (Ch. 6).

**Tacit Management Knowledge** — The unwritten rules of negotiation, political context, cultural nuance, and professional standards that govern success in a leadership role. When learned informally, it exacerbates inequities (Ch. 4).

**Technical Excellence** — Mastery of the specific, functional tasks of a job (data, code, protocols) (Ch. 1). It is the passport to promotion but does not predict leadership success (Ch. 5). *See also: Technical Competence*

**Teleology** — A consequence-based ethical framework stressing outcomes such as harm prevention, service quality, and maximizing public trust. Mandates selecting a candidate who is demonstrably ready (Ch. 9). *See also: Deontology*

**Ten Days of Leadership Reflection** — The structured self-reflection guide (Appendix A) designed to help readers internalize the core lessons of each chapter and apply them to personal leadership practice (App. A).

**Transfer of Learning** — The process of verifying that skills learned in a developmental program (Level 2) are consistently applied as observable behavioral changes back on the job (Level 3) (Ch. 6). This is the key metric for multimodal development (Ch. 4).

**Upward Managing** — The failure pattern where a favored or unprepared leader prioritizes pleasing the appointing authority (their boss) over setting priorities and supporting their own team (downward leading). This creates echo chambers where dissent cannot rise (Ch. 3).

**"Wicked Problems"** — Complex, systemic challenges endemic to public service (e.g., homelessness, climate adaptation) that resist traditional linear, analytical solutions. They require leaders with non-linear competence and cultural intelligence (Ch. 4).

## How to Use This Glossary

This glossary is designed as both a reference and a learning tool. Students and practitioners can use it to clarify key terms while reading, or as a framework for reflection when applying leadership principles in real-world settings. Instructors may also use glossary terms as prompts for discussion, written reflection, or applied case analysis.

# Appendix A - Ten Days of Leadership Reflection: Applying the Lessons of Promoted into Incompetence

**How to Use This Guide**

This ten-day reflection guide is designed to help readers internalize the lessons of *Promoted into Incompetence* by translating insight into action. Each day corresponds to one chapter and invites a pause for deliberate reflection on how the ideas apply to your leadership practice—or to the practice of leaders you have observed.

Set aside twenty to thirty minutes per day. Read the **Key Insight**, reflect on the **Prompt**, and complete the **Action Exercise** in writing. If possible, keep a dedicated notebook or document so you can revisit your reflections as your leadership evolves.

## Day 1 - The Confidence-Competence Gap

**Key Insight:**
Technical excellence is not the same as leadership readiness. Confidence often gets mistaken for competence, yet effective leadership depends on humility, awareness, and the ability to deliver results *through* others.

**Reflection Prompt:**
When have you—or someone you've known—been promoted based more on confidence or visibility than genuine readiness? What happened next?

**Action Exercise:**
List three indicators of *true readiness* for leadership in your organization. Circle the one most often overlooked and note one way you could make it more visible in your own practice.

## Day 2 – The Real Costs of Misaligned Leadership

**Key Insight:**
Leadership misalignment produces both visible and hidden costs—lost trust, burnout, turnover, stalled innovation, and eroded public confidence.

**Reflection Prompt:**
Think of a time when weak or misaligned leadership drained energy or resources in your team. What were the tangible and intangible costs?

**Action Exercise:**
On a sheet of paper, draw two columns labeled *Operational Costs* and *Human Costs*. Fill in examples from your experience. Identify one step you could take today to reduce or prevent one cost in either column.

## Day 3 – Systemic Drivers of Incompetence (Part I)

**Key Insight:**
Three forces commonly elevate the wrong people into leadership: merit systems that overvalue technical testing, internal promotion cultures that equate seniority with readiness, and favoritism that rewards likability over competence.

**Reflection Prompt:**
Which of these systemic forces is most visible where you work? How does it shape perceptions of fairness or morale?

**Action Exercise:**
Write a brief paragraph proposing one structural fix—policy, training, or culture change—that could reduce the influence of that force.

## Day 4 - Systemic Drivers of Incompetence (Part II)

**Key Insight:**
Even well-designed systems fail when organizations neglect mentoring, succession planning, and management education. "They'll figure it out" is not a leadership strategy.

**Reflection Prompt:**
Who mentored you—or failed to—when you first led others? How did that presence or absence shape your development?

**Action Exercise:**
Identify one emerging leader around you. Note one concrete way you could mentor, coach, or prepare that person within the next thirty days.

## Day 5 - Technical Excellence ≠ Leadership Competence

**Key Insight:**
Doing the work well differs fundamentally from leading others who do the work. Leadership demands communication, delegation, vision, and accountability—the "long-distance muscles" of organizational success.

**Reflection Prompt:**
What technical strengths might hinder your ability to delegate or empower others?

**Action Exercise:**
Choose one project where you tend to stay too close to the details. Outline a plan to delegate one part of that project to another team member and schedule a feedback discussion after completion.

## Day 6 – Building Leadership Pipelines with Intention

**Key Insight:**
Intentional pipelines prevent accidental promotions. Succession planning, cross-training, and mentorship create readiness instead of relying on luck or seniority.

**Reflection Prompt:**
Does your organization treat succession planning as preparation or as replacement?

**Action Exercise:**
Sketch a quick pipeline for one critical role in your department. List at least two potential successors and one development experience each would need to be ready.

## Day 7 – Tools for Emerging Leaders

**Key Insight:**
Leadership growth accelerates through coaching, feedback, and stretch assignments that build new skills under guidance, not through trial by fire.

**Reflection Prompt:**
When have you grown most as a leader—through success or through discomfort?

**Action Exercise:**
Design your own "stretch assignment." Write three sentences describing what it would involve, what you hope to learn, and who could support you as you take it on.

## Day 8 - Changing the Story

**Key Insight:**
Awareness and intention are the antidotes to the leadership trap. Recognizing systemic problems and committing to act differently are the first steps toward change.

**Reflection Prompt:**
What habitual belief or assumption about leadership in your organization needs to be challenged?

**Action Exercise:**
Write a short statement beginning with "From now on, I will…" that captures a single intentional change you want to embody in your leadership approach.

## Day 9 - The Ethics of Leadership Misalignment

**Key Insight:**
Promoting without preparation is not just inefficient—it is unethical. Ethical leadership requires fairness, stewardship, and accountability for the well-being of teams and communities.

**Reflection Prompt:**
When has a promotion decision you observed raised ethical questions about fairness or readiness? How was it handled?

**Action Exercise:**
Review the eight principles of the ASPA Code of Ethics. Write one sentence for each describing how it applies to leadership selection in your context.

# Day 10 – Final Call to Action

**Key Insight:**
Organizations and individuals share responsibility for competent leadership. Leadership is learned, not assumed.

**Reflection Prompt:**
After reading *Promoted into Incompetence*, what one insight has most changed the way you view leadership transitions?

**Action Exercise:**
Draft your personal **Leadership Readiness Plan.**
List three leadership competencies you want to strengthen, one learning resource or mentor for each, and a realistic timeline for progress. Conclude with a short paragraph titled "My Commitment" summarizing how you intend to lead with awareness and intention.

## Closing Note

These ten reflections are a starting point. Leadership development is not a sprint of ten days but a continual practice of self-examination and adjustment. Return to these prompts periodically, especially when facing new transitions or mentoring others through theirs. Each reflection represents both a safeguard against being *promoted into incompetence* and a step toward the kind of intentional, ethical leadership public service needs most.

# Appendix B - The Leadership Alignment Project

An 8-Week Portfolio for Emerging Leaders

**How Appendix B Complements Appendix A**

Appendix A invites reflective practice over ten days—internalizing each chapter's core lesson and applying it personally. Appendix B is the applied counterpart: an eight-week, field-based Leadership Alignment Project that asks emerging leaders to observe a real organization, diagnose systemic drivers of leadership misalignment, assess ethical and competency gaps, and design practical interventions. Together, they turn insight into practice (Appendix A) and improvement (Appendix B).

## Overview and Intent

This project helps leaders in training connect the book's ideas to the realities of public, healthcare, and nonprofit organizations. Over eight weeks, you will build a Leadership Alignment Portfolio that blends observation, analysis, ethics, and design. The tone is professional and developmental; you can complete it individually or in a cohort/learning circle.

- Duration: 8 weeks (works as a midterm or end-of-term capstone in a 16-week course, or as a focused professional development sprint).

- Output: A four-part Portfolio—Observations, Diagnostics, Reflections, Recommendations.

- Sectors: Prompts include examples and 'sector tags' for public administration, healthcare administration, and nonprofit leadership.

Ethics & Confidentiality: Do not collect sensitive or personally identifiable information. Anonymize organizations, people, and data. If your setting requires permission to observe or interview, obtain it; otherwise, rely on public sources and your own experience.

## What You Will Produce (Portfolio Components)

1. **Observations**: A brief organizational snapshot and process map for how leaders are selected, trained, and supported.
2. **Diagnostics**: Two driver-analysis tables (Ch. 3–4), a Competence vs. Readiness Matrix, and a stakeholder map.
3. **Reflections**: Short memos connecting observations to human and ethical implications.
4. **Recommendations**: A practical intervention (policy, pipeline, training, or ethics safeguard) plus a one-page implementation roadmap.

At the end, you'll assemble these into a polished Leadership Alignment Portfolio (see the 'Portfolio Assembly & TOC' section).

## Week-by-Week Guide (8 Weeks)

Each week focuses on a specific stage of analysis and portfolio building. The cumulative process ensures both understanding and application.

### Portfolio Assembly & Suggested Table of Contents

1. **Cover Page** – Title, your name (or cohort), organization anonymized, date.
2. **Executive Summary** (2–3 pages): Crisp narrative of findings and proposed intervention.
3. **Observations**: Role Snapshot, Process Map, Observation Log, Stakeholder Map.
4. **Diagnostics**: Driver Tables, Competence vs. Readiness Matrix.
5. **Reflections**: Ethics & Equity Memo, Personal Learning Reflection.
6. **Recommendations**: Intervention Brief, Implementation Roadmap.

7. **Appendices** (Optional): Templates, additional notes, anonymized artifacts.

## Templates (Ready to Use)

This project employs six practical templates that help structure your observations and analysis. The templates are designed as **clean, print-ready tables** and include sample entries illustrating their use.

1. **Leadership Observation Log** (Week 2) – tracks key moments and leadership behaviors.
2. **Stakeholder Map Worksheet** (Week 2) – identifies internal and external stakeholders and their influence.
3. **Driver Diagnostic Tables (Parts I & II)** (Weeks 3–4) – assess how the five systemic drivers appear in your organization.
4. **Competence vs. Readiness Matrix** (Week 5) – compares technical expertise with leadership preparedness.
5. **Ethics & Equity Checklist** (Week 6) – applies the ASPA Code of Ethics to promotion and readiness processes.
6. **Implementation Roadmap** (Week 7) – outlines milestones, ownership, and timeframes for your proposed intervention.

*Detailed, fillable versions of all six templates appear in **Appendix C: Leadership Alignment Templates.***

## Closing Note

The Leadership Alignment Project is designed to cultivate judgment, not to produce a single 'correct' answer. Your value as a leader grows when you can (1) see the systemic drivers that promote people into misalignment, (2) recognize the ethical and equity stakes, and (3) design practical interventions that build readiness. Use this portfolio as both a learning record and a springboard for real improvements—in your team, your organization, and your own leadership practice.

# Appendix C – Leadership Alignment Templates

These templates accompany Appendix B – The Leadership Alignment Project and are designed to help emerging leaders capture observations, analyze data, and plan interventions. Each template includes a sample entry to demonstrate its use. They may be copied, printed, or adapted for individual or classroom use. All examples are illustrative; replace them with your own observations.

## Template 1 – Leadership Observation Log (Week 2)

Use this table to record leadership behaviors, decisions, or interactions you observe. Focus on what happened, what leadership behavior you saw, and the effect on people or outcomes.

| Date | Setting /Meeting | What Happened | Leadership Behaviors Observed | Impact/Implication |
|---|---|---|---|---|
| 3/4/2025 | Budget review meeting | Manager delegated budget preparation to analyst and reviewed results together. | Collaboration; coaching; shared accountability. | Increased analyst confidence; improved accuracy of final report. |

# Template 2 – Stakeholder Map Worksheet (Week 2)

List internal and external stakeholders and assess their level of influence and interest. Add short notes on their needs or potential concerns.

| Stakeholder | Internal/External | Influence (1–5) | Interest (1–5) | Key Needs/Risks/Concerns |
|---|---|---|---|---|
| Finance Director | Internal | 5 | 4 | Requires timely financial reports; concerned about audit preparation. |
| Community Advisory Board | External | 3 | 5 | Wants transparency and inclusion in planning discussions. |

| Driver | Presence (Low–High) | Impact (Low–High) | Evidence / Examples |
|---|---|---|---|
| Merit system structures overvaluing technical exams | High | High | Exams focus on technical skills, not leadership readiness. |

| | | | |
|---|---|---|---|
| Promotion from within based on seniority | Medium | High | Internal postings emphasize tenure; leadership criteria limited. |
| Favoritism/ personal preference | Low | Medium | Some appointments made on personal trust rather than qualification. |

# Template 3 - Driver Diagnostic Tables (Parts I & II, Weeks 3-4)

Evaluate how systemic drivers appear in your organization. Rate each for presence and impact, then provide short evidence or examples.

Part I - Structural Drivers (Ch. 3)

Part II - Support Drivers (Ch. 4)

| Driver | Presence (Low–High) | Impact (Low–High) | Evidence/Examples |
|---|---|---|---|
| Lack of training and mentorship | High | High | No structured onboarding or coaching program. |
| De-emphasis of management education | Medium | Medium | Limited PD funds; management courses optional. |

# Template 4 – Competence vs. Readiness Matrix (Week 5)

Plot candidates or current leaders based on technical competence and leadership readiness. Use notes to interpret placement.

|  | Low Leadership Readiness | High Leadership Readiness |
|---|---|---|
| High Technical Competence | At risk of promotion into incompetence – delay + develop. Example: Senior analyst with strong technical skill but limited management experience. | Promote/empower with supports. Example: Coordinator who mentors peers and leads cross-functional projects. |
| Low Technical Competence | Not ready – clarify role and expectations. | Potential fit for coordination roles with technical oversight. |

| Criterion | Meets Standard (Y/N) | Notes / Evidence |
|---|---|---|
| Transparent process | Y | Posting and scoring criteria shared with all applicants. |
| Fair access to opportunity | N | Internal candidates prioritized; external posting delayed. |

| | | |
|---|---|---|
| Leadership competencies included | Y | Interview rubric evaluates communication, budgeting, and supervision. |
| Safeguards against favoritism | Y | Panel diversity ensured; documentation retained. |
| Mentorship offered equitably | N | Training only provided post-selection. |
| Social equity considerations addressed | Partial | Limited outreach to underrepresented groups. |

## Template 5 – Ethics & Equity Checklist (Week 6)

Apply ethical and equity principles to assess fairness and transparency of a promotion or leadership transition.

## Template 6 – Implementation Roadmap (Week 7)

Use this roadmap to track milestones, ownership, timing, and risks for your proposed intervention.

| Milestone | Responsible Party | Start Date | Finish Date | Notes / Risks |
|---|---|---|---|---|
| Design mentorship framework | HR Director | 5/1/2025 | 6/15/2025 | Requires executive approval and minor budget. |
| Pilot mentorship program | HR & Dept Leads | 7/1/2025 | 9/30/2025 | Track participation and satisfaction. |
| Evaluate outcomes & expand program | HR Analytics | 10/1/2025 | 12/31/2025 | Use survey and turnover data to evaluate success. |

## Closing Guidance

Use these templates as living documents—revise, expand, and revisit them as your understanding of leadership alignment grows. Together with Appendix B, they form a complete diagnostic and development portfolio for leaders in public, healthcare, and nonprofit organizations.

# References

Allen, T. D., & Eby, L. T. (Eds.). (2010). *The Blackwell handbook of mentoring.* Blackwell.

ASPA (2013). Code of Ethics. American Society for Public Administration.

Bandura, A. (1997). *Self-efficacy: The exercise of control.* W. H. Freeman.

Bidwell, M. (2011). Paying more to get less: The effects of external hiring versus internal mobility. *Administrative Science Quarterly, 56*(3), 369–407. https://doi.org/10.1177/0001839211433562

Boyatzis, R. E. (2018). *The competent manager: Model for effective performance.* Wiley.

Braga, G. T. (2020). Is public administration struggling in higher education? Evidence from the United States scenario. *Teaching Public Administration, 38*(2), 105–121.

Bridges, W. (2009). *Managing transitions: Making the most of change.* Da Capo Press.

Cascio, W. F. (2006). The economic impact of employee behaviors on organizational performance. *Academy of Management Perspectives, 20*(3), 124–128.

Chamorro-Premuzic, T. (2019). *Why do so many incompetent men become leaders? (And how to fix it).* Harvard Business Review Press.

Charan, R., Drotter, S., & Noel, J. (2011). *The leadership pipeline (2nd ed.).* Jossey-Bass.

Cooper, T. L. (2006). *The responsible administrator* (5th ed.). Jossey-Bass.

Day, D. V., & Dragoni, L. (2015). Leadership development theory and research. *The Leadership Quarterly, 26*(1), 20–38.

Day, D. V., Gronn, P., & Salas, E. (2004). Leadership capacity in teams and organizations. *The Leadership Quarterly, 15*(6), 857–880.

Denhardt, R. B., Denhardt, J. V., & Blanc, T. A. (2013). *Public administration: An action orientation (7th ed.).* Wadsworth.

Dweck, C. S. (2006). *Mindset: The new psychology of success.* Random House.

Edmondson, A. C. (2018). *The fearless organization: Creating psychological safety in the workplace for learning, innovation, and growth.* Wiley.

Fraser, D. E. (2025, September 18). *Promoted into Incompetence? The Leadership Trap We Don't Talk About Enough* (slides and speaker notes). COMPA Webinar.

Gabarro, J. J., & Kotter, J. P. (2005). Managing your boss. *Harvard Business Review, 83*(1), 92–99.

Getha-Taylor, H., Jensen, C., Perry, J. L., Wright, B. E., & Moyle, M. (2011). Leadership development for public managers: Capacity-building in state and local government. *Public Administration Review, 71*(6), 882–889.

Goleman, D. (1998). *Working with emotional intelligence.* Bantam.

Heifetz, R. A., & Linsky, M. (2017). *Leadership on the line: Staying alive through the dangers of change* (Rev. ed.). Harvard Business Review Press.

Higgs, M., & Rowland, D. (2010). What does it take to implement change successfully? *Journal of Applied Behavioral Science, 47*(3), 309–335.

Hill, L. A. (1992). *Becoming a manager: How new managers master the challenges of leadership.* Harvard Business School Press.

Hogan, R., & Kaiser, R. B. (2005). What we know about leadership. *Review of General Psychology, 9*(2), 169–180.

Ibarra, H. (2015). *Act like a leader, think like a leader.* Harvard Business Review Press.

Ingraham, P. W. (1995). *The foundation of merit: Public service in American democracy.* Johns Hopkins University Press.

Ingraham, P. W., & Getha-Taylor, H. (2005). Leadership in the public sector: A review of academic and practitioner perspectives. *Review of Public Personnel Administration, 25*(1), 58–75.

Kellough, J. E., & Nigro, L. G. (Eds.). (2006). *Civil service reform in the states: Personnel policy and politics at the subnational level.* SUNY Press.

Khatri, N., & Tsang, E. W. K. (2003). Antecedents and consequences of cronyism in organizations. *Journal of Business Ethics, 43*(4), 289–303. https://doi.org/10.1023/A:1023081629529

Kidder, R. M. (1995). *How good people make tough choices.* Harper Collins.

Kirkpatrick, D. L., & Kirkpatrick, J. D. (2016). *Evaluating training programs (4th ed.).* Berrett-Koehler.

Kruger, J., & Dunning, D. (1999). Unskilled and unaware of it: How difficulties in recognizing one's own incompetence lead to inflated self-assessments. *Journal of Personality and Social Psychology, 77*(6), 1121–1134.

Lewis, D. E. (2008). *The politics of presidential appointments: Political control and bureaucratic performance.* Princeton University Press.

Maslach, C., & Leiter, M. P. (2022). *The burnout challenge: Managing people's relationships with their jobs.* Harvard University Press.

Maslach, C., & Leiter, M. P. (2022). *The burnout challenge: Managing people's relationships with their jobs.* Harvard University Press.

Méndez, F., & Sepúlveda, F. (2016). A comparative study of training in the private and public sectors: Evidence from the United Kingdom and the United States. *Contemporary Economic Policy, 34*(1), 107–118.

National Civil Service Reform League. (1937). *The civil service in modern government: A study of the merit system.* New York, NY: Author.

National Archives. (1883). *Pendleton Act (1883).* https://www.archives.gov/milestone-documents/pendleton-act

OECD Council. (2019). *Recommendation on Public Service Leadership and Capability.* https://legalinstruments.oecd.org/en/instruments/OECD-LEGAL-0445

Office of Personnel Management. (2007). *Assessment decision guide.* https://www.opm.gov/policy-data-oversight/assessment-and-selection/reference-materials/assessmentdecisionguide.pdf

Office of Personnel Management. (2012). *Structured interviews: A practical guide.* https://www.opm.gov/policy-data-oversight/assessment-and-selection/structured-interviews/guide.pdf

Office of Personnel Management. (n.d.). *Assessment & evaluation: Leadership assessments.* https://www.opm.gov/services-for-agencies/assessment-evaluation/leadership-assessments

Office of Personnel Management. (n.d.). *Executive Core Qualifications (ECQs).* https://www.opm.gov/policy-data-oversight/senior-executive-service/executive-core-qualifications

Pearce, C. L., & Conger, J. A. (2003). *Shared leadership: Reframing the how and why of leadership in organizations.* Sage.

Peter, L. J., & Hull, R. (1969). *The Peter Principle: Why things always go wrong.* William Morrow.

Plant, J. F. (2018). Responsibility in Public Administration Ethics. *Public Integrity, 20*(sup1), S33–S45. https://doi.org/10.1080/10999922.2017.1413927

Raelin, J. A. (2016). *Work-based learning: Bridging knowledge and action in the workplace.* Jossey-Bass.

Reid, W. M., & Dold, C. J. (2017). Leadership training and the problems of competency development. *Journal of Public Health Management and Practice, 23*(1), 73–80.

Rittel, H., & Webber, M. (1973). Dilemmas in a general theory of planning. *Policy Sciences, 4*(2), 155–169.

Rousseau, D. M. (1995). *Psychological contracts in organizations: Understanding written and unwritten agreements.* Sage.

Svara, J. H. (2014). Who are the keepers of the code? Articulating and upholding ethical standards in the field of public administration. *Public Administration Review, 74*(5), 561–569. https://doi.org/10.1111/puar.12230

Schmidt, F. L., & Hunter, J. E. (1998). The validity and utility of selection methods in personnel psychology. *Psychological Bulletin, 124*(2), 262–274.

Seidle, B., Perry, J. L., & Fernandez, S. (2016). Do leadership training and development make a difference in the public sector? A panel study. *Public Administration Review, 76*(4), 603–613.

Senge, P. M. (2006). *The fifth discipline: The art and practice of the learning organization.* Doubleday.

Spencer, L. M., & Spencer, S. M. (1993). *Competence at work: Models for superior performance.* Wiley.

Sorkin, A. R. (2018, October 23). 'Paul Volcker, at 91, Sees a Hell of a Mess in Every Direction.' *The New York Times.* https://www.nytimes.com/2018/10/23/business/dealbook/paul-volcker-federal-reserve.html?auth=link-dismiss-googletap

Spillane, J. P. (2006). *Distributed leadership.* Jossey-Bass.

U.S. Code. (n.d.). *5 U.S.C. § 2302 Prohibited personnel practices.* Cornell Law School Legal Information Institute. https://www.law.cornell.edu/uscode/text/5/2302

U.S. Merit Systems Protection Board. (2019). *Preserving the integrity of the federal merit systems: Understanding and addressing perceptions of favoritism.* https://www.mspb.gov/studies/studies/Preserving_the_Integrity_of_the_Federal_Merit_Systems_Understanding_and_Addressing_Perceptions_of_Favoritism_945850.pdf

U.S. Office of Personnel Management. (2023). *Leadership assessment report* [Report]. Retrieved from https://www.opm.gov/services-for-agencies/assessment-evaluation/leadership-assessments/

U.S. Office of Special Counsel. (2024). *Your rights as a federal employee* (handout summarizing Prohibited Personnel Practices). https://osc.gov/Documents/Outreach%20and%20Training/Handouts/Your%20Rights%20as%20a%20Federal%20Employee%20(v2024).pdf

White, R. C. (1942). [Review of History of the Federal Civil Service, 1789 to the Present]. *Social Service Review, 16*(3), 590–592.

Wilmerding, L. (1935). *Government by merit: An analysis of the problem of government personnel.* New York: McGraw-Hill.

Work Institute. (2023). *2023 Retention Report.* Work Institute.

# About the Author

**David E. Fraser, Ed.D., MPA,** is a distinguished scholar-practitioner, executive leader, and educator whose career spans more than three decades across government, higher education, and the nonprofit sector. His work bridges theory and practice, emphasizing the ethical, strategic, and human dimensions of organizational competence.

Dr. Fraser currently serves as Chief of Staff to an elected official in Contra Costa County, California, where he has spent nearly twenty years overseeing legislative strategy, fiscal policy, and departmental operations across one of the Bay Area's largest and most complex counties. His leadership career also includes senior executive roles with the City of Oakland, Volunteers of America Bay Area, and the New York Urban League, reflecting a deep commitment to mission-driven administration and cross-sector collaboration.

As a member of the graduate faculty at California State University, East Bay, Dr. Fraser has taught for two decades in both the Master of Public Administration (MPA) and Master of Science in Healthcare Administration (MS-HCA) programs. His courses span public management, ethics, organizational change, budgeting, and research methods, equipping emerging leaders with the tools to translate theory into effective practice.

Dr. Fraser earned his Doctor of Education (Ed.D.) in Higher Education Leadership and Master of Public Administration (MPA) in Public Management, integrating academic inquiry with the realities of executive decision-making. This dual grounding informs his examination of how technically skilled professionals often rise to leadership roles without adequate preparation for the human and systemic challenges of management—an issue at the heart of *Promoted into Incompetence*.

A member of the Institutional Review Board at Cal State East Bay, Dr. Fraser also belongs to the American Society for Public Administration (ASPA) and the National Society of Leadership and Success (Sigma Alpha Pi). Through Fraser Leadership Group, he continues to mentor emerging leaders, advance ethical governance, and promote evidence-based strategies for organizational excellence.

www.ingramcontent.com/pod-product-compliance
Lightning Source LLC
Chambersburg PA
CBHW070625030426
42337CB00020B/3912